MUSIC PRODUCTION
2024+ EDITION

Limit
6
7
8
9
10
11
12

MUSIC PRODUCTION 2024+ EDITION

Published 2023 by Tommy Swindali

DISCOVER "HOW TO FIND YOUR SOUND"

https://www.subscribepage.com/tsmusic

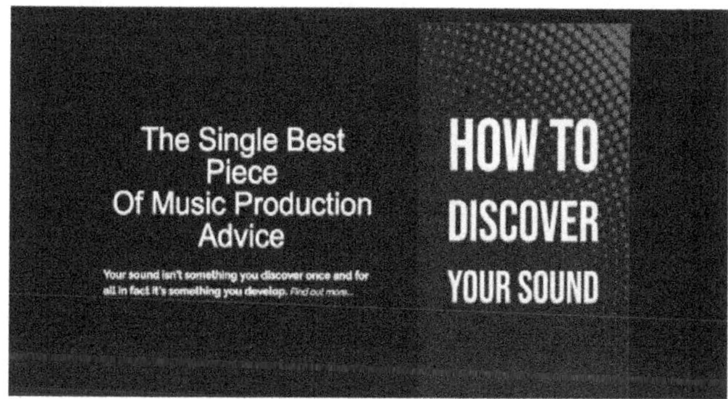

Scan the QR code for more.

CONTENTS

MUSIC PRODUCTION FOR BEGINNERS | 2024+ PRODUCTION

MUSIC PRODUCTION | 2024+ PRODUCTION

MUSIC PRODUCTION FOR BEGINNERS | 2024+ EDITION

INTRODUCTION

Why do some albums stand the test of time throughout the decades? How were they produced? What exactly did those famous musicians go through before their hit songs were heard on the airwaves? These are most certainly among the questions you ask yourself as you hear the biographies of the music artists you highly admire and look up to.

As you delved through those artists' backstories, you might have learned that plenty of them are home-based, DIY musicians who, after plenty of attempts and after going through multiple sets of trials-and-errors, have finally broken through to the pinnacle of the mainstream scene of popular music.

Inspired by their success, you are strongly considering trying your luck as well. You believe you are just as talented as they are. So if they made it, then perhaps you will too. But then, there are "higher powers" that you need to please: rich, influential people that you need to appease, hoping they will open the portal that will propagate your musical artistry among the masses.

Those people have standards, which are oftentimes impossible to meet. Since you do not want to compromise your artistic expression just to please them, you resorted to doing things on your own. You decided to invest in affordable equipment, learn how to use some free downloadable audio software, and hope that the knowledge and skills you need to finally make it as a musician will just bestow themselves upon you, as you go along mastering your craft.

But then, a huge array of obstacles started to appear: complex technical processes that you need to go through, scientific concepts that you need to comprehend, and all sorts of virtual and physical tweaking that you need to execute. Furthermore, you figured out that they should be done in perfect balance for the sake of producing an impressive musical output that, hopefully, would captivate the listening public.

As a passionate musician, this is a huge burden that needs to be addressed. Lucky for you, the remedy is here in your hands… you're holding it right now.

It Is Not as Difficult as You Think

Around two decades ago, there was absolutely no other way for music artists to achieve widespread fame apart from recording a demo tape, submitting it to a record label, and waiting for the approval of the higher powers mentioned earlier (AWAL, 2019). Should they be lucky enough to get the attention of those higher powers, they will be given enough funding to record their songs in a studio, work with audio engineers to make an impressive output, and compile their songs into an album that their record label would then sell to the public.

Such a process is so painstaking that the great majority of aspiring artists quit while just halfway through the project. Back then, plenty of musical attempts were a "one step forward, two steps back" kind of endeavor. The technical, financial, and business aspects of record album production were just so massive that many artists just threw in the towel while admitting that they were not just meant to make it.

But then, software technologies for recording sound began to sprout here and there, which were quickly picked up by music enthusiasts. A few more years of developing and polishing those technologies went by, and fast-forward to these present times, when anyone with the artistry and willingness can make studio-level music tracks right in the convenience of their own bedroom!

This does not mean that music production at home can be done totally for free, though, unless of course if you have some existing equipment already. You still need to invest in some quality equipment because, after all, a high-quality output is what you are actually aiming for.

Thankfully, the equipment needed for it does not have to be very expensive. The truth is, for a few hundred dollars, you can set up a mini-home studio, and come up with a very professional-sounding song that people would have difficulty believing was produced at home.

As you attain more financial rewards from your efforts, you might then be urged to buy more expensive gear for the sake of improving your craft, or for the sake of rewarding yourself with a higher level of personal satisfaction. This is a part of the journey that all successful music producers went through.

What you have to bear in mind though, is that having a huge budget is not a necessity in the early stages of the journey you are now taking. As long as people perceive your song to be catchy and lovely enough, they won't care how that song was recorded or where it was produced.

All they care about is the beat, the melody, and the captivation they got from it—all those technical and complex processes would certainly amount to nothing once they get mesmerized by your symphony. As you delve into the coming lessons, you will eventually agree how true this is.

Why Should You Bother Reading Further?

With more than 24 book titles under my belt, I have played as a DJ with famous music artists in the UK and produced music for plenty of high profile entities and events. With years of experience as a producer, I've achieved success as a best-selling author with highly reviewed books on Amazon, Kindle, Apple Books, and nearly every online publishing platform you could think of.

Aside from music production, I have also published books about music theory, instrument mastery, and other topics pertaining to what's really going on behind the music industry. Since my textbooks and audiobooks have all been very well-received, you can be certain that as you educate yourself on the topics that follow in the next chapters, you'll benefit from my track record and authority on the subject.

A lot of benefits await you if you immerse yourself in the technical and artistic indoctrination that lies ahead. Whether you're an indie artist who struggles to be heard or a serious musician who wants to make a living out of your talents, you will be ushered into the ins and outs of home music production and what it takes to step out into the bigger arena. How you should collaborate with other entities to further your fledgling music career will be discussed as well.

You will also learn how music production in the digital age is actually conducted and the underlying processes that you need to familiarize yourself with. Because of the presence of computerization, these processes are simplified to the point that you can do them without obtaining any formal education in them at all.

With the lessons you will learn as you read further, it will not matter if you are a solo performer, a member of a huge band, or a DJ who utilizes digital technology to mesmerize crowds. Regardless of your goals or music genre as a music producer, this book has a lot in store for you.

From recording to arranging to mixing and mastering your tracks, the intricate processes will be discussed in an in-depth manner with the essence of simplicity. This is to make sure that you, as an aspiring mainstream musical artist or producer, will get the help you need to finally attain that career status you have been desperately aiming for.

If your love for music has grown cold recently, flip through the pages and be ready to fall for your first love once more. Be ready to immerse yourself in the ecstatic dimensions of music production!

CHAPTER 1
BECOMING A DIGITAL-AGE MUSIC PRODUCER

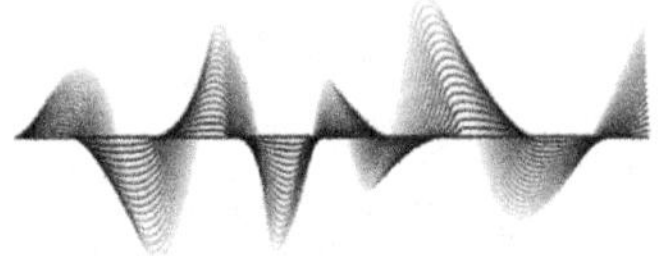

You are on a journey to learn how to produce music at home. It's probably all you think about and want to talk about. You've probably searched Google endlessly for instructions on how to do it. Well, your search is over, because the answer is now in your hands.

You probably hate pitching your music ideas to big-time record producers, who will most likely just turn you down—if they ever have time to listen to your creations at all. You want to become your own artist, your own performer, and your own promoter, who will put out all the effort… and reap all the rewards. Achieving such status means you have to be able to record music at home, edit it on-the-fly, and publish your creations for the whole world to see, without the intervention of any all-knowing mega-rich deity.

You want to be a self-made, modern-day record producer, and you should feel entitled to reach the pinnacle of this dream. Well, here's the good news: You have every right to be! In starting this rather ambitious journey, there is a mental conditioning regimen you have to go through, and it includes internalizing the following directives.

Having The Right Skills and Mindset

Success comes with a price. You may need to pay for that success with a bit of money, but the far greater cost for you will be in terms of patience, hard work, and persistence. Added to those are the pressures and failures that show up along the way, which will present themselves as obstacles before you finally attain the success you highly desire. If we were to sum it up, you need to have the proper mindset and skills to become a digital-age music producer.

Having the right mindset means being able to learn and acknowledge certain realities in the music production business. If you have not yet grasped that the success you hear about from the music icons you idolize is just the tip of the iceberg, now should be the time to start grasping it.

Needless to say, hard work is a key element in being good at this endeavor you are about to start. So, to put it bluntly, this is a journey you do not want to embark on if laziness and procrastination are among your most common traits.

Let us assume that you have already gotten over that part. Now, you have to embrace another harsh truth in this field—that we need to attain some skills, particularly on the technical side of things, so that we can record music, polish it, and bring it out into the world so people can hear it.

Such skills can be learned from others, but the bulk of them may come from our own mistakes and failures. Even in the field of music production, the saying "Experience is the best teacher" still holds true. You need to motivate yourself for self-education and have the discipline needed for it. There will be countless moments when you will have nothing but yourself to rely on, so be prepared for that as well.

You must also learn how to connect with others who have been there before you, and utilize their wisdom to your advantage. This is the most important mindset you have to attain, before everything else.

Thriving Through Networks

As you might have guessed, hopping into this field is mostly about recording audio and finalizing your output so it can be ready for audiences. But that is just one facet of the process; there is a much larger consideration, which involves getting through the right platforms so people can have access to your music.

You might not want to accept this part, but there is a business aspect to music production (Pastukhov, 2019). This is a necessity to keep you going and allow you to earn proficiently. It is understandable that passion is the main reason why you are venturing on this journey. But focusing on passion alone is not a realistic approach–you need to accept that there are other factors at play that you need to be a part of as well.

Such factors involve connecting to other people of similar interests, knowing how to collaborate with them, and figuring out how to execute plans and solutions to get things done. It would be wonderful to imagine things going smoothly in accordance with your personal preferences. Sadly though, it does not always work like that.

There are people you need to please, and there are business expectations that you need to meet. This will be part of the cycle you will go through, for each and every musical project you work on. Your tasks will not always be based on your tastes and desires because there are other people who have different tastes and artistic styles.

Because such a notion is undeniable, you have to thrive through networks—in the real world and the online world as well. Today, the virtual dimension is getting wider and more accessible as each minute passes. You have to use it to your advantage by reaching out to people so you can work with them and sell your services to them.

The good thing about propagating your music online is that you don't have to meet all of your collaborators in person. There will be plenty of times when you will be conversing with them by phone, through a video call, or just via emails.

However you may choose to get in touch with your industry partners, one thing is for sure—you need to communicate with them. Without a clear exchange of messages, projects would not get done, payments wouldn't be sent, and your business would not thrive. You have to embrace this and start internalizing the fact that as a music producer in the digital age, this is something you must sincerely do along with your main avenue of writing and perfecting your music, your true passion.

Knowing the Right Tools

Like a painter who knows exactly what kind of brush and paint to use while working on a canvas, an aspiring music producer like you should also learn about the best tools of the trade, so you can put them into practice. Thankfully, there are plenty of such tools scattered all over the internet.

As someone who is just starting out, a great deal of your time should be spent reading through countless forums, reviewing blogs, or listening to discussions about the matter. This requires you to get emotionally and mentally invested, as a stream of trials and errors will certainly come your way.

This is where your patience will be first tested—you need to learn how one tool is better than another or if those experienced music producers are right in their claims that this tool or that tool is the best that the industry could and should offer.

A lot of these self-proclaimed experts would show some level of "arrogance and self-entitlement" that you might have a hard time dealing with, so, as stated earlier… patience. For the sake of gaining the knowledge necessary to pick and use the right tools, you have to make an exhaustive list of your prospects, sort them out, and scratch off the ones that you deem unnecessary for your needs. Once you have done that, you have to start learning how to use them right away.

Most of these tools will belong to the software category, so we have to assume you already have some background in software interface manipulation. If you are not well-versed in it yet, then it would be very wise to start listening to online discussions about such lessons as soon as you can.

In addition to digital tools, you will also need certain pieces of equipment. You need not worry about huge expenses, though, because we are here in the digital age, where even the most expensive electronic devices appear in plenty of brands and models. If you look long and hard enough, you will be surprised that there are lots of them that are sold in the market with surprisingly cheap price tags.

Digital Audio Workstations: Why You Should Learn These Software Tools

The world today is so modernized that finding a workplace without any computerized systems is very unlikely. In that regard, it is absolutely impossible that you would find a recording studio that does not rely on computer systems to capture sounds, rectify errors, and tailor them to suit audiences' tastes and preferences. Everywhere you look, computerization is present, and without its help, it is impossible to attain the precision and perfection that we as imperfect humans so fiercely desire.

Having said that, you have to embrace the idea that your computer-related knowledge and your adeptness in manipulating software interfaces are skills you will have to enhance. You need a computer to become a proficient music producer, or even if your ambition is to be a simple home-based musician aiming to release music independently.

To officially start your journey on either of those two closely related paths, you need to make a vital choice. This is about picking the right DAW (Digital Audio Workstation). This is a software tool that will let you record the vocals and instrumentation that will one day become that hit song you hope will propel you to stardom. Picking your DAW is a meticulous process (Huff, 2021). It has to be, since your overall mood every time you record and arrange your music will be highly dependent on that very choice you made.

Choosing your DAW and How to Quickly Adapt to It

Choosing the right software tool to get the job done is like finding a needle in a haystack—there are literally endless lists to choose from! We can either blame or thank the internet for this. To get right to it though, we should rather thank the web instead of blaming it. So how should you choose your DAW? Or better yet, what is the best one that experts recommend?

Truth be told, there is no definitive right or wrong answer to this. The more accurate questions to ask should sound like this: Will that DAW address your music production needs in the most beneficial manner? Is the interface easy enough to navigate for a beginner like you? Can your music projects be seamlessly imported into other similar software?

As you seek the answers to these questions, you might eventually find out that more questions will present themselves, which would surely complicate the situation even more. Let us simplify it then. We might just do that by separating the free software from the ones that require payment.

The best free DAW applications include:

- **Audacity:** known to be very lightweight and easy to use

- **MixPad:** offers very easy editing by means of dragging and dropping
- **Ocenaudio:** allows fast audio editing without using too much computer memory
- **GarageBand**: enables professional-level audio editing in a streamlined manner
- **Tenacity:** the closest competitor of Audacity, very ideal for novices

If you find it too troublesome to check each one of them out, you should pick Audacity outright—a lot of experts recommend it because of the simplicity and ease of use it offers (Lendino, 2022). But here is the thing about free stuff: it lacks the versatility and editing prowess that the paid ones can provide.

Among the best-recommended ones used by professionals are:

- **Ableton Live:** ideal for DJs and live digital music performers
- **FL Studio:** ideal for music mixing that includes videos
- **Apple Logic Pro:** best for mixing natural-sounding music
- **PreSonus Studio One:** ideal for live performances and typical mixing tasks
- **Steinberg Cubase:** known for its fast, and very easy-to-use MIDI editor

If you want to fully unleash your music production potential in an unparalleled way, you should definitely explore DAWs that experts in the field today are using or those that are categorized as "industry standards" (Rogerson, 2023). Since experts love to endlessly preach about how one software tool is better than the other, the safest route to head for as a beginner should be those free software tools mentioned above. After spending some time working around them, you should easily identify which among the payable categories suits your recording needs best.

Understanding the Basic DAW Setup

The process of browsing the web for that ideal DAW is very painstaking; there is no doubt about it. For that reason, a simplified way of understanding the basic "standard anatomy" of a typical DAW is something that you have to rightfully attain. Though DAWs are basically perceived as purely software-oriented in nature, a DAW in the context of music production is actually comprised of 3 basic components:

- **An audio interface:** where you will plug your microphone or musical instrument.
- **A computer:** a desktop or laptop where you will plug your audio interface.
- **An audio editing software:** the software enumerated previously: Audacity, FL Studio, MixPad, etc.

There should be no need for a lengthy explanation about the type of computer to use. Literally any standard functioning computer will serve the purpose of accommodating the software you need, storing your recorded data, and mixing your tracks, which will eventually be transformed into the songs that comprise your albums.

But for the sake of formality, let us get acquainted with the typical specifications that constitute an ideal computer where you will work on your music along with your DAW. This is a typical list of minimum computer specs:

- Memory : 8 GB of RAM
- Storage : 500 GB HD space
- CPU : 3.50 Ghz

Eight gigabytes of RAM (Random Access Memory) is today's standard for average desktop and laptop computers. A speed of three gigahertz or more for the CPU (Central Processing Unit) is also very common among the most recently released models. These two specs are mainly the main factors that affect the speed of a computer: how fast it loads or how fast it performs its overall tasks (Christian, 2022). The 500 gigabytes of hard disk space refers to the storage space you have to store your sound files.

Since audio processing is not as resource-hungry as video processing, buying any standard computer out there on the market today would perfectly serve your recording needs. Even with that old laptop you bought several years ago, you can still install some high-end DAWs that most professionals use today.

For storing your sound recordings, you might want to invest in an external hard disk drive, which is technically just an extra storage device that you can plug into a USB port. This is to accommodate the backup routine you might occasionally do. Mixing and equalizing can be a very lengthy and painstaking process. It is strongly recommended that you store and back up your mixed projects properly in case something goes wrong with your computer system or if your DAW becomes inaccessible due to system bugs and crashes.

Some music producers work with massive monitors and talk about them like they are a necessity. But since we are dealing with sound production here, we can safely say that big screens are worthless add-ons. For the audio component of your system, though, a good pair of high-end speakers is a must. Thankfully, a big budget is not needed for this.

Good headphones, which are also very affordable, are something to have too. They must be present along with your speakers, so you can carefully differentiate (and appreciate) varying sound and frequency levels. When arranging and mixing your tracks, there will be times when you need to hear them from large, loudspeakers in full blast. There will also be special moments when you need to listen to them with smaller, more intimate devices such as headphones. This is something we will discuss further in the chapters ahead.

DAW Navigation: Basic Skills You Have to Learn

We have already established that there are plenty of DAWs out there to choose from. While each one of them offers different features and interface layouts, the general framework from which they can be manipulated is basically the same. This is great news for anyone who believes that working with a DAW means dealing with extreme difficulties in mastering the craft.

Since the functionalities of most DAWs are practically the same, it would be wise to attain some kind of "generalized mode of DAW manipulation." To easily grasp how your chosen audio software tool works, or how to operate any possible DAW you might soon hop into, you must ingrain your brain with the following elements that typically comprise a standard DAW interface.

Menu Bar

This contains all the commands, functions, and features of your DAW. Like most software you are already familiar with, it appears as a horizontal bar with the familiar "File, Edit, View, etc." menu items. Of course, not all DAWs are arranged that way, but most certainly, they are equipped with a menu bar that appears on the topmost portion of the screen. It looks very similar to all the other menus of all the software applications you may think of.

Transport Toolbar

This one is easy to spot because it resembles the "Play, Pause, Stop, Record" buttons that we often see on every record player. They function exactly like those buttons that you are so familiar with while listening to your favorite albums on cassette, CD, or any known tangible record player you may think of.

Tools Toolbar

Choosing various tools such as cutting, pasting, and zooming are all visible here. Additional default settings include volume adjustment, time-shifting, and track insertion. The default icons and features on it could greatly vary depending on your DAW, but most likely, the features mentioned here will be present there.

Recording Meter

This is the conventional name for the section of the DAW that displays either a glowing green or red bar. If green is visible most of the time, it means your audio level is in an ideal setting and that you have nothing to worry about. If it turns orange, it means the audio being recorded is about to get clipped or distorted. It is not recommended that you wait for it to turn red—this indicates clipping—before decreasing your recording volume.

Playback Meter

Typically situated next to the recording meter, this indicates the volume level of the tracks you are playing while mixing. The green and red displays also apply as you interpret the loudness of your tracks. Unlike the levels displayed in the recording meter, though, this does not affect the quality of the final output of your recordings.

Mixer Controls

Often identifiable by the mic and speaker icons on them, they are used to set the level of your recording device (your microphone or instrument) and the loudness of your playback. They are used to control the recording meter and the playback meter, respectively.

Device Toolbar

Choosing the devices to be recorded, like the microphone or any instrument plugged into your audio interface, happens here. Typically, those devices will be displayed as a drop-down list where you can choose the name of the device that will be the source where you want to record sounds from. Also, the playback device where you want to hear the recording can be chosen here, like if you want to hear it from your speakers or if you want to hear it from your headphones.

Timeline Bar

This is where you can see the rate at which the tracks you are mixing are played. By zooming in or out on your tracks, you will see that the timeline adjusts accordingly, as it shows the length of your tracks in minutes, seconds, or milliseconds.

Waveform Window

Conventionally called "waveforms," this is the actual workspace of all DAWs. Basically speaking, you could refer to it as your text document if you were working with a word processor. Here, you can see the actual graphical representation of your tracks. If a certain portion of your track is very loud, it appears as a huge wave. Conversely, it appears as a small wave if it is recorded at a low volume.

Control Track Panel

Usually placed on the left of your waveforms, this is where you set the volume levels of the left and right channels of your track. This is also where you tweak if you want your mono tracks to be merged into stereo. Some more advanced DAWs offer better flexibility on their control track panels, which could include equalization, sound effects, and other tools for polishing your tracks.

Regardless of the brand name of your DAW, the features mentioned above would most likely be present on its interface. If you can learn how to move around them and grasp how they work, you can have the guarantee that you can easily hop from one DAW interface to another without much hassle.

Working With Your DAW and Making the Most Out of It

The next thing to learn about is what you will actually do with your chosen DAW. As you have read previously, your DAW is your main tool where you will record the vocals and instrumentation parts of your song. So what you will be seeing most of the time is the workspace area of Audacity, FL Studio, or any of the similar software mentioned above.

Working with your DAW can be summarized into four steps:

- **Importing/recording tracks:** making them visible and ready for editing and mixing.
- **Editing/mixing:** modifying and enhancing tracks, making them cleaner and more pleasant to hear.
- **Mastering:** setting the frequencies of each track, so they would meet industry standards.
- **Exporting:** finalizing the overall audio project, making it ready for the audience.

Regardless of the DAW you pick, your tasks will most likely revolve around these four steps. Importing and exporting requires no lengthy explanation since your computer will mostly do the task for you, apart from inputting file names and assigning folder locations where your tracks will be saved. But mixing and mastering are very complex procedures, which we will explain in detail in the next chapters.

Once you hit the record button, you will see waveforms moving bigger or smaller, depending on the loudness or softness of your sound's source. You will then use the tools in your DAW's menu to do the editing necessary to make your recorded tracks sound the way you want them to.

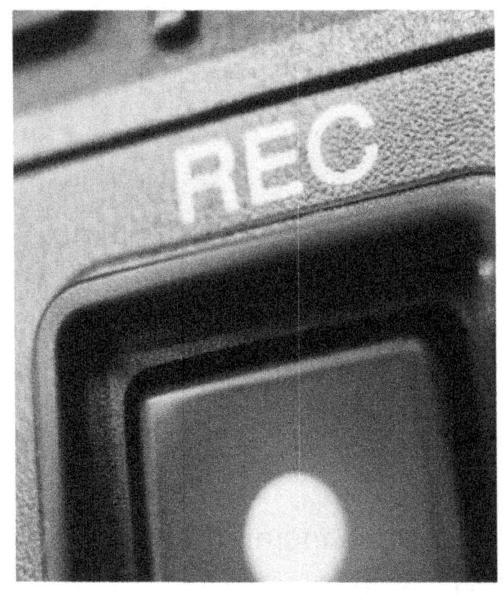

Aside from recording tracks, importing them is also something you will do. There is nothing difficult about this, since all you will be doing is dragging some chosen tracks and dropping them into your workspace. Your DAW will automatically display the waveforms of those tracks, and you should be able to edit them right away.

Importing may take a while to load, depending on the size and number of those tracks. File types are generally not an issue since any DAW you choose will most likely support standard file types such as FLAC, ACC, MP4A, MP3, and WAV.

WAV is the industry standard and the most commonly used sound file format. You must prioritize it over any other sound files. It does not mean, though, that the other ones mentioned above are not that good. The advantage of using WAV is that it retains all the original frequencies of a recorded sound, so during compression or any other audio processing tasks, the properties that make your sound authentic will stay as they are (Adobe, 2023).

For convenience, and particularly to maintain high fidelity,

WAV is the format you should choose to save your sound files. This will make it convenient for others to work on your audio projects as well. Likewise, it would also be much easier for you to work with artists who might hire you to enhance the music they recorded somewhere else.

Utilizing Add-ons, Updates, and Plug-ins

Your chosen DAW contains plenty of features and add-ons that will greatly help to make your job easier. You have to find time to explore them as well, since utilizing them will help you bring about more polished and unique sound outputs. For instance, in mixing your vocals, your DAW might already contain equalizer presets that you can simply click and apply to your tracks.

These presets can really get the job done much quicker because they are settings made by professional sound engineers. For sure, these settings would not sound too bad when applied to your projects. In cases where you do not like how those presets sound, you may do just a little fine-tuning on your own.

This takes some time to develop since your ears, as a newbie, will not be able to distinguish various sound and frequency differences for the first few tries. Patience is something you really have to learn in this phase.

From time to time, the software manufacturer that made your DAW will provide notifications of their latest updates, and you should keep your software up-to-date in order to best serve the purpose you hope to achieve. These updates could be bug fixes, plug-ins, or additional features that could be useful, or they could simply be marketing strategies that you might find very annoying. The safest bet for this would be downloading those updates every three months or so, because anything more frequent than that would not make much difference from the current version you are using.

With each passing year, DAWs are getting better and have become much easier to use over time. This is good news for us. We only have to acquire a few bits of knowledge about software manipulation, and the very best DAW out there could be ours for the taking.

CHAPTER 2
BASICS OF HOME RECORDING

Based on what we've tackled so far, it should be clear by now that as a music producer or indie artist, what you will be mostly doing is recording, arranging, and mixing. At this point, let us understand the basics of recording instruments and vocals, the two main components that comprise most songs. Whether you are recording an acoustic or piano-accompanied song, or if a full band is required, there will generally be two main sessions in the recording process of every song: instrument recording and vocal recording.

If you are a novice music producer who takes your newfound career very seriously, you should understand that the process we are about to discuss is not simply about putting someone's mouth near the microphone and hitting the record button. It is not also about simply plugging in a guitar and letting some knobs and buttons do the work for you. There is a definitive science to how things are done in this area. But thanks to software technology, it is not as complex as you might have thought it would be.

Understanding Sound: Wavelength, Frequency and Amplitude

Hopping into the actual recording process without understanding the basic principles of sound is unwise, so let us discuss them a bit in this section. When illustrated graphically, we could picture sound traveling in the shapes of mountains and ditches, so, basically speaking, it would be best to describe sound as a series of waves.

Understanding how sound travels can be done by observing a loudspeaker. As you hear music playing through it, you can see that it moves up and down at varying speeds. As the speaker moves, air molecules are pushed outward from it in rapid pulses. They would then travel to our ears, where they would then be interpreted as sound by our brains.

In order for a certain stream of pulses to be actually perceived as sound, they must happen plenty of times per second, or they will not be heard at all. This means that in order for a certain kind of sound to be heard, it has to reach a certain level of frequency in order to be perceived.

Human ears are known to capture only frequencies between 20 Hz and 20,000 Hz. Anything lower than 20 Hz is subsonic, while anything above 20,000 Hz is supersonic. What this implies is that anything higher or lower than these frequencies would be sounds that no human will ever hear (National Park Service, 2018).

Since sound travels in waves, it is also important to understand how vital wavelength is to sound recording. A longer wavelength indicates fewer pulses, which means a lower pitch is captured.

Conversely, a shorter wavelength indicates more pulses, meaning a higher pitch is obtained.

Wavelengths also have transverse waves, which are referred to as the height of the sound waves. When viewed graphically in your DAW, you can figure out that the length of the transverse waves determines the amplitude or volume of a high-pitched or low-pitched sound.

As you conduct your recording sessions, wavelength, frequency, and amplitude are sound elements you will deal with all the time, regardless if you are recording vocals or instruments. You might find this too overwhelming, but you should find great comfort in the notion that if you can understand how to operate your DAW pretty well, the intricate science behind sound will be scaled down to a level that you and I can easily comprehend.

Recording Methods and Techniques

By now, it is assumed you have already learned how your chosen DAW works and how to find your way around it whenever a recording session happens. As you begin to capture melodies from your vocal cords or from those of other singers, and as you record the tunes and vibrations from your chosen instruments, the following techniques and methods are ones you should apply.

Soundproofing (or at Least Having the Next Best Thing)

The best musical recordings are crisp, clean, and impeccable—these are the primary adjectives that should describe the output of your music production. While it is natural that raw recorded vocals and instruments do not sound very good initially, polishing them to perfection is very difficult (if not impossible) if they are recorded with plenty of unwanted noises in the background.

Unless a certain kind of sound element is required in the audio project you are working on, your microphone or recording device must never capture anything else aside from the voice of the singer or the raw, plain sound of the instrument you are recording. This is the reason why music studios are soundproofed—they are designed to record every sound element in the cleanest and purest way possible.

So the question is, do you really need a totally soundproof room? As a novice music producer, no—not yet anyway. Instead of building an expensive room with thickly-insulated walls, you might want to consider building a vocal booth instead. It appears like a phone booth or a chamber big enough for a human singer to fit into. Most vocal booths can be built with materials that cost roughly between $600 and $800 (McAllister, 2021).

If you find that too much of an expense, you might use a vocal isolation box instead. It functions as a vocal diffuser as you sing or speak through the microphone. It is nearly three times the size of a standard shoebox and is lined with sound diffuser padding on its walls, which prevents your mic from capturing the unwanted reverb from the walls of your session room.

Another advantage it offers is that it filters out the noise behind your microphone to some degree as well. As long as there are no direct sources of extreme noise behind the singer, a vocal isolation box works wonders for most DIY musicians that cannot afford to build a soundproof room just yet.

Of course, a vocal box does not always lead to a totally noiseless recording. It can, however, lead to crisp recordings inside the right rooms during the right moments of the day. There are times when the neighborhood or your house itself is not too noisy, and you should find a way to take advantage of that.

If you have scoured through DIY music blogs and videos all over the internet, you might have learned already that there are plenty of "bathroom musicians" out there. If you have not come across their kind, let us just say that they are labeled as such because they recorded many portions of their music inside a bathroom.

Obviously, the bathroom is most likely the smallest room with the smallest window in your house. However, the natural reverb in most bathrooms is entirely unsuitable for making a clean recording. On the other hand, recording inside a closet can work very well, as the clothing acts as natural soundproofing. You might want to consider doing this as well.

Whichever works for you, or if you have other facilities in the house where you can place your vocal isolation box conveniently, you should use it. The point of using a vocal box is to diminish the background noise to a level that it is almost non-discernible during the recording process.

There might still be some little noises, but your chosen DAW can work its magic and remove those unwanted sound elements, which is something that we will discuss in the next pages. A wise newbie music producer knows how to utilize the resources and best moments to make music, and you should not think too differently regarding this matter.

Learn Appropriate Mic Placement (and How to Pick the Right Ones)

But how about recording instruments? Would vocal isolation boxes be usable for that? Sadly, no, not usually. But there is a remedy for that, and it has something to do with the kind of microphone you will use. In most studios everywhere, there are basically two kinds of microphones: the dynamic mic and the condenser mic.

A dynamic mic is what you should use if you are recording an acoustic guitar, a piano, or any unplugged instruments such as percussion. By placing it in front of your guitar, it can capture that specific sound without capturing other noises in the background.

Dynamic mics are also ideal if you are recording vocals with a band, as this type of mic only captures the voice of the singer or a single instrument in close proximity. If you are singing with a dynamic mic, your mouth must not be farther than six inches from the mic so that you can get the best possible input from your own voice.

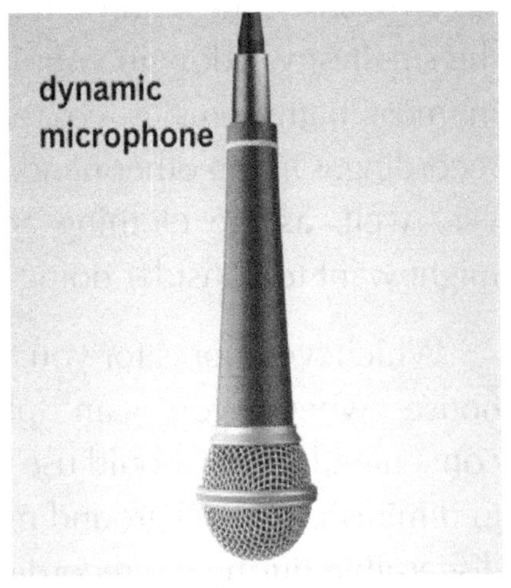

If you want your voice to sound as natural as possible, you should use a condenser mic. It is regarded by audio engineers as "more honest" than all other types of microphones out there. They are viewed as such because they can accurately capture the natural inflections that your lips, your tongue, and all the other body parts you use when singing.

The downside with condenser mics is that they can capture distant sounds—even a dog barking a few blocks away could enter your recording. This is the reason why the soundproofing lesson you learned earlier should be taken seriously.

In most home or professional studios, condenser mics are often preferred when recording vocals over dynamic mics. So to put it simply, dynamic mics are ideal for instruments, while condenser mics are for human voices. This does not mean, though, that you can never use dynamic mics for vocal recording. If you find it more ideal for your voice recording needs, then nobody should dictate to you that one mic is better than another.

When using either of the two, there are techniques you need to apply to get the best possible vocal recording. As was mentioned earlier about dynamic mics, you need to be as close to them as possible to make your voice clear enough for capture. Since distance is a major issue when using it, you must not stand too far away from it.

With a condenser mic, you can be meters away from it or just a few inches away. This highly depends on your singing style or the kind of sound you want to achieve. But the problem with singing very close to a condenser mic is that an undesirable kind of sound might be picked up, especially in syllables that start with "B" and "P."

As a remedy, a pop filter should be placed between your mouth and your mic. It is simply a wide plastic ring with a cloth mesh in the middle. It is typically made using nylon mesh, the same material used in ladies' stockings. No doubt you have seen these in the music tutorial videos you have looked into. With a pop filter, your inflections while singing with a condenser mic will sound much better since the unwanted sound of air from your mouth will be filtered out.

Another technique worth considering is placing your mic at eye level. This would make you tilt your head a bit upward, which would generate more vocal power as you sing. This is just a tip, though, and should roughly depend on your personal preferences.

Your choice of mics and how you place them can really make a huge difference in how your music will be perceived by the audience. Make sure you spend enough time choosing and using them—they can really make or break your song production career while you are just starting out.

Work on Your Rhythms and Record Them First

In the realm of music, timing is everything. Whether you are up there onstage, playing alone in your room, or singing along with a song played over the radio, being rhythmic is what makes people hooked on music. Perfectly executed rhythms are a must for each and every music track you record. It is the reason why, in every song recording session, most record producers implement a solid rule: work on the rhythm section first.

This means that when recording with a full band, the drums and the percussion must be dealt with first. The bass guitar would typically come next, then the rhythm guitar, then the solos or the harmonics (Grushecky, 2022). While there is no solid rule as to what instrument comes after the drums, the vocals would typically come last. It is the track that delivers the real message of the song. Naturally, the voice of the singer is often given the greatest focus because, after all, it is what the song will be most notably recognized for.

There are also record producers who choose to record the vocals right after all the instruments of the rhythm section have been recorded. Some instrumental soloists prefer to overlay their riffs and licks with the highs and lows of the vocalists. In that case, they ask for the vocals to be recorded first before recording their intricate guitar or piano solos.

Of course, nothing is etched in stone about how you should conduct your recording sessions. There is nothing illegal about refusing to record the drums last, nor would it violate any constitutional laws if you do not include the bass guitar in the final stages of your recording. But if we were to ask any experienced music producer out there, recording the rhythm section first is a drill followed by the very best in the music industry for generations.

"If it ain't broke, don't fix it," so the saying goes. So if that rule has been making recording sessions so smooth long before you were born, you should not try to defy it and risk ruining your dream of recording some of the best tracks ever.

Use a Metronome or a Drum Machine

But what if a lone music producer cannot play drums or any percussion instruments? What if they only want to record an acoustic or piano-laden track? What if an a cappella track is all that is required for a project? In that case, obviously, no drum tracks are recorded. However, the artist must still adhere to a series of predefined beats provided by a metronome.

In music production, the clicking sound of a digital metronome is an indispensable tone that all professional musicians highly rely on. Because of its accuracy in producing very precise time signatures, the possibility of getting out of time as you follow a metronome is very unlikely, unless, of course, if you do it intentionally. If you set a metronome to generate 93 beats per minute, it will continually do so for eternity, unless you hit the stop button or if your DAW shuts down for some reason.

Metronome beats are there to help musicians stick to a very consistent playing speed. In cases where drum parts are not required for a song, the guitarist, pianist, or any accompanying musician will record their tracks while listening to the clicking sound of a metronome. This is a standard procedure in music production, one thing you have to be familiar with (MasterClass, 2022).

If you hate the monotonic clicks of a metronome, you might want to utilize something more interesting, something that techno artists and rappers are so fond of using: drum machines. With such an electronic rhythm device, you can program certain beats in accordance with a predefined time signature. You can stitch it together into loops and let it play over and over throughout the entire duration of the recording.

Compared to the monotonous sound of a metronome, the beats from a drum machine are richer and more dynamic. It gives you the option of a snare drum, a bass drum, cymbals, and everything else a real drum kit provides—and more. Plenty of DIY musicians, club DJs, and those that consider themselves a "one-man-band" find drum machines to be their best friend.

The great thing about drum machines is that they are not only instruments for rehearsals; they can also be used in actual recording sessions. This might come as a surprise to you, but plenty of the hit songs you hear these days, especially songs with really complex drum beats and drum fills, do not actually employ real human drummers during recording. This is one of the wonders of recent digital innovations—some musicians are now replaced by software technology.

Record the Fills and Harmonies

If you are confident already with how your beats and rhythms are recorded, it should be the time for harmonies and fills to join the fray. Harmonies can be simply defined as "anything that makes your song more flavorful." Strings, backup vocals, and other sound effects you may think of incorporating into your song belong to this category.

Plenty of major-label music producers employ orchestras and choirs to blend harmonies into their tracks. This is a brilliant idea, of course, but as a home-based music producer, you are not there yet, right? So instead of going through that huge expense, you might just consider using the sound effects that your keyboard generates or those plug-ins offered by your DAW.

Another tool to utilize is an electronic keyboard. Today, the most ordinary one you may already have can synthesize hundreds of sounds. For sure, it can generate the sound of a violin, a cello, or even the sound of a huge choir. Such effects are so easy to utilize and are absolutely free. You have to make use of them for the time being until you are capable of paying for a concert orchestra in your makeshift studio.

Guitar fills, bass fills, and other additional instrument tracks should also be done in this phase. In recording distorted electric guitar sounds, you have to be aware that it is more complicated to record than other instruments. This is because guitar distortion has a very wide variety of textures and could introduce too much noise in your overall output. So in recording guitar solos, along with the distorted rhythm guitar mentioned previously, a much tighter discipline is required. Frequency isolation is needed for this, which is something we will discuss deeper in the next chapters.

Understanding Preamps and Audio Interfaces

Having a crisp and clear audio output has been mentioned repeatedly throughout our discussions, which means we have to be dead serious about having it. There are other devices you must have to achieve the recording perfection you so highly aim for. In this section, let us get acquainted with preamps and audio interfaces.

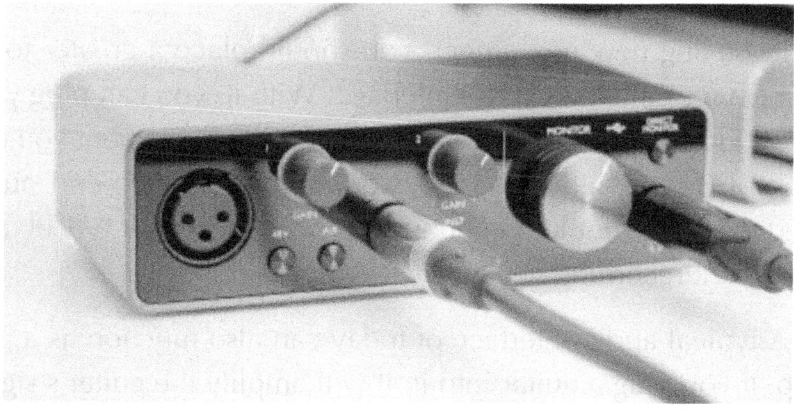

Simply put, a pre-amp is a device that you can use to amplify weak signals without accumulating distortion. If you want to boost your microphone's signal, you can do that by simply turning up the volume level in your DAW. But the problem with that approach is that it would degrade the quality of your mic's sound, thereby ruining the sound quality.

But with a pre-amp, you can enhance the ideal signal that your microphone harnesses and boost it while retaining the crystal clarity that the natural sound of your mic is capable of. If you have existing, old-school analog equipment, you might just as well utilize them since they would sound good enough as long as they have withstood the wear and tear through the years. And if you have instruments with weak signal outputs but still want to use them in your recording, a pre-amp will come in handy for retaining sound quality.

But if you have some more recently-bought equipment, it is most likely already designed to work well with the prevalent sound devices of today. Most probably, they already have a built-in preamp in their circuits, so you do not have to worry about understanding the concepts that make them work. For instance, most DJs and techno music performers today use turntables and synthesizers with preamps built into them.

In buying new equipment, you should place a greater focus on a device called an audio interface. With it, you can plug your mic, your guitar, your keyboard, or any other instrument you can think of. For as little as $100, you can buy a high-end audio interface that should be enough to cater to your vocal and instrument recording needs (Truss & Corfield, 2021).

A typical audio interface of today can also function as a pre-amp. If you plug a guitar into it, it will amplify the guitar's signal to ideal levels that should be clean and comprehensible enough for your computer to interpret. That raw sound would then be processed in your DAW, so it can be transformed into whatever sound format you highly desire.

Pre-amps could have as few as two input jacks, or they could be as many as 18, depending on the brand or the model. While starting out, a double input device should be enough for you, as it will be all you need to record one vocal and one instrument. You have to also bear in mind that unless you are capturing a live performance, a multi-track recording is rarely done in home studios such as yours.

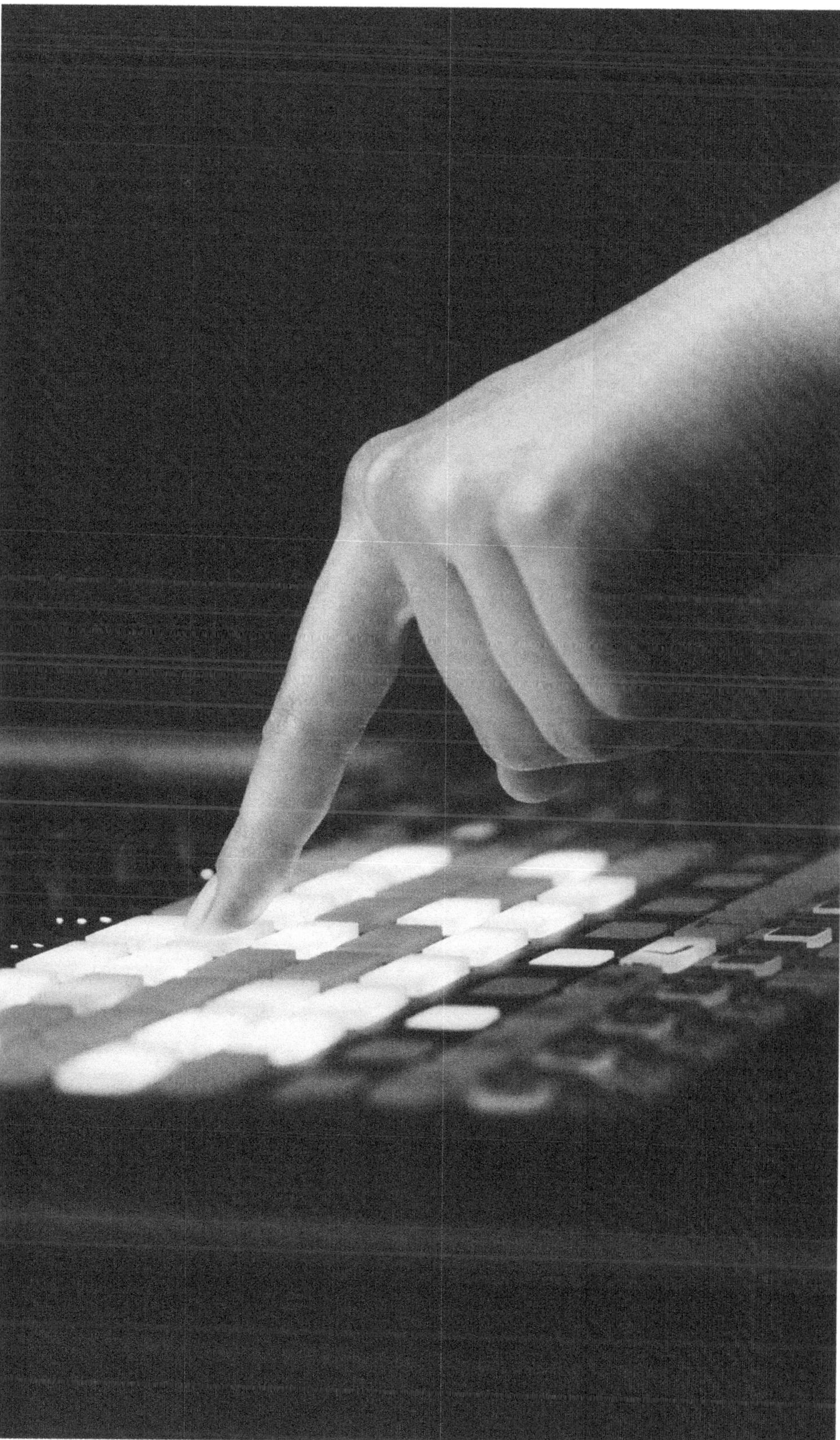

CHAPTER 3
MIDI AND VIRTUAL INSTRUMENTS

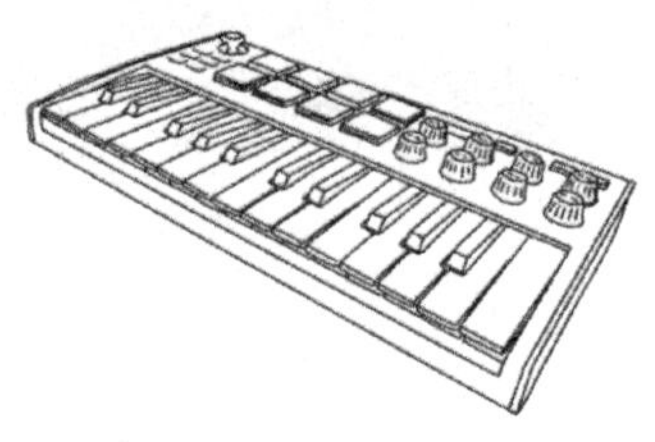

It was mentioned in the previous chapters that computerization is highly involved in every aspect of our modern lives. Even in the field of music, which is supposed to require only the most disciplined and artistic minds, plenty of the relevant processes in its creation need the involvement of computer simulation.

The likes of Beethoven, Mozart, and Bach might not be pleased that musicians today do not rely anymore on the skills of their hands or the precision of their minds, but music nowadays is done this way. We need virtualized instruments and even virtualized environments in music production.

Without the existence of computer-simulated music elements, it would be very difficult for even the most talented musicians to keep up with the rapid-paced demands of today's music industry. With that being said, let us now educate ourselves on MIDI and virtual instruments and see for ourselves how applicable and helpful they really are in our tasks as a music producer.

The Evolution of MIDI to VSTI

MIDI (Musical Instrument Digital Interface) can be simply defined as "rendering music in a digital way." During the 1980s,

MIDI was introduced as an actual port where musicians could plug synthesizers so that musical notes could make their way to computer memory in digital form.

Though MIDI as an architecture was first introduced in 1983, it was not until 2013 that inventors Ikutaro Kakehashi and Dave Smith received Technical Grammy Awards for their achievement (Stewart, 2021). Because of the inclusion of MIDI in computer systems, the way music is produced and published was forever changed.

Because of MIDI, even non-musicians can create music that is indistinguishable from that performed by very talented artists. Drum machines, as mentioned previously, are the most popular instruments in the MIDI category. Its kind has now become truly indispensable for music producers everywhere, in every possible music genre you could think of.

MIDI started as an actual physical port where a musical instrument could be plugged in and communicate with a computer. Such a breakthrough led to the eventual creation of VST (Virtual Studio Technology), which virtualizes a studio setting within a computer system.

To put it simply, VST was truly responsible for miniaturizing a huge studio because it can now appear on a desktop as a computer simulation. Over the years, VST further evolved into VSTI—a much more complex system where music enthusiasts can play instruments in a simulated manner.

Nearly every possible musical instrument you can imagine now has a VSTI version of some sort: piano, guitar, horns, strings, and even an entire orchestra for that matter. Even an entire studio or a massive concert hall can now be simulated virtually because of this technology. Without a doubt, MIDI made music production a lot easier and, not to mention, a lot more fun.

Because MIDI evolved into VSTI, solo performers can now be heard like a full band onstage. DJs can now mesmerize huge crowds in clubs much more dynamically. With a few tweaks of a VSTI, certain genres in electronic music, such as house, trance, and techno, can be executed instantaneously.

Today, all music artists, regardless of their status, can unanimously agree that without MIDI, it is impossible to appease the modern tastes of music-hungry fans all over the planet. It cannot be denied that people today easily get bored. Even for very passionate artists like us, our attention spans have become undeniably shorter. Because of this reality, music creators must adapt to the modern trend of producing music in the speediest manner possible.

Since we can all agree that people are very eager to hear and see something new every time they browse the web, a much quicker way of producing music must be implemented as well. Clearly, there is no better method or tool out there than a computer with MIDI capabilities, along with the virtual instruments that come along with it.

Basics of Programming VSTIs

Like knowing the basics of working with DAWs, working with virtual instruments is a skill every digital-age music producer must possess. Because virtual instruments function through automation, they must be programmed so they can work seamlessly with the other instruments that are present in your song.

One of the most vital figures you have to input in

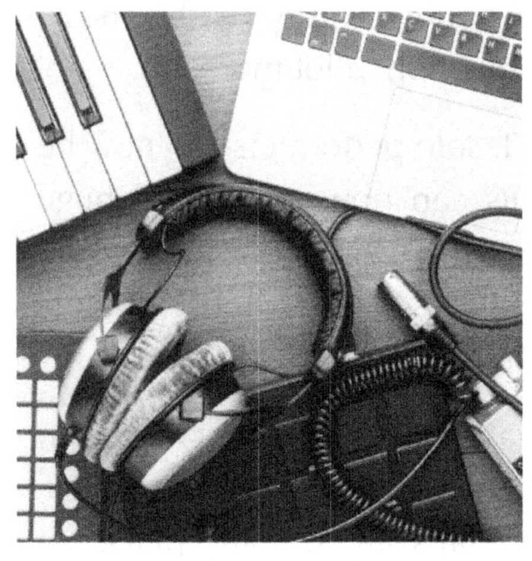

programming virtual instruments is the number sequence that determines the rhythm pattern of your song. For instance, you might be prompted by your chosen virtual instrument's interface to key in the time signature of your song if it is in 2/2, 3/4, 4/4, etc. You would then input how fast the song would be by keying in the number of beats per second.

Most virtual instruments today are so graphically detailed that you will be presented with an actual illustration of an instrument on screen, and you can play them by tapping into their parts with your fingers or through your mouse. Even how they are strummed or struck can also be programmed, though this might greatly vary depending on what kind of instrument is presented.

Another vital piece of information to input would be the chord pattern or progression of your song. Programming this would require you to input how long a chord should be played in seconds or milliseconds. As long as you enter appropriate values, your virtual instrument will never skip a beat and will provide accurate accompaniment no matter how long you use it for recording or rehearsal.

Categorized VSTIs You Must Strongly Consider

Should you decide to use virtual instruments in crafting your music, consider the following VSTIs. Here is a list of VSTIs classified in accordance with common instrument categories.

Guitars:

- IK Multimedia AmpliTube 5
- Positive Grid BIAS Amp 2 Elite
- Valhalla Supermassive

Bass:

- IK Multimedia MODO Bass
- Heavyocity Scoring Bass
- Ample Bass Guitar

Strings and Orchestra:

- VSCO 2 Chamber Orchestra
- DSK Overture/Brass
- Sonatina Symphonic Orchestra

Drums and Percussions:

- Alesis Stereo Electronic Drum Machine
- StudioLinked Drum Pro
- Spitfire LABS Drums

For DJs and Live Techno Performances:

- Rekordbox,
- Virtual DJ
- Ableton Live

If you scour the web, you can find endless lists of VSTIs. Rest assured, the ones mentioned above should be enough to cater to your most common music production needs. Some VST applications are so versatile that you could even make your own personalized virtual instruments within them, and you may program them according to your own predefined rules.

This works by recording each and every key or note of any

instrument you may want to virtualize. Though this might be a laborious process you want to avoid, this is something you have to be aware of because such a demand might arise from your future clients.

Artificial Intelligence: The Decline of Real Musicianship?

VSTI made plenty of musicians' lives easier than ever. But from the perspective of some artists, the fact that music is "too automated" these days removes the real sense of artistry that music is meant to possess. A lot of old-school musicians openly express their disgust over younger artists who make music using their computers. But the truth is that for the public, the process of making music does not really matter. If it sounds good to their ears, then it is acceptable. And if they like listening to it, then it is worthy of the popularity it has attained.

Because of the clever collaboration of computer programmers and sound engineers, a musical revolution has emerged with a superstar called "Artificial Intelligence." The inclusion of AI in music production initially started with the mere creation of pre-defined beats that musicians could use to bring about a very accurate kind of playing.

Over the years, though, AI's participation has evolved into simulating fake pianos, fake horns, and fake orchestras. As the decades went on, AI became a chord pattern generator, melody consultant, and musical error analyst! Because of this, plenty of traditional musicians have ever-growing fears that one day their jobs might be taken away by computers and robotic performers.

As a music producer of the digital age, maybe you cannot help but ask, "Are those old-school musicians right? Would the tasks of a sound engineer, or even the careers of today's most famous music icons, be abolished because of AI?" Nobody has a definitive answer at the moment. But as a music producer of the modern age, you might just as well utilize what AI has in store for you.

Instead of grumbling about how modern music creators are less-talented than the ones in the past, let us just be grateful that with computer technology, our jobs as entertainment personnel have become a lot more convenient. Because of AI's presence in the field of music production, music studios are now miniaturized and have made their way into our homes at an affordable price.

Because computers have made it so much easier for aspiring music creators to learn the craft, the entire avenue of music publishing can be shared by every willing soul. Gone are the days when only the rich, the powerful, and the influential could build music studios, so they could benefit exclusively from the fame and glory of musicians with very promising talents.

Because AI exists, the act of recording, enhancing, and releasing your music is accomplished in half the time and at a fraction of the cost. Older musicians might hate us for loving AI, but instead of resorting to endless arguments regarding the matter, let us just accept the reality that virtual instruments are here and will most likely remain to make life easier for decades to come.

Using Virtual Instruments to our Advantage

It is clear based on what we have learned so far that getting rid of MIDI and virtual instruments is very unlikely. The best thing to do then would be to put them to use in order to enhance our music. Understanding their benefits will help us leverage their advantages. We have given an overview of how they work, but let us dig into them a bit deeper. Here are some of the greatest benefits of using virtual instruments.

Less Manpower is Required

Though it might appear as bad news for traditional musicians, virtual instruments can benefit a music producer by removing the need to have real human musicians in a studio. Instead of hiring a real violinist to play with you as you strum your guitar, you can program a virtual instrument with some predefined chord patterns. As you play your parts in accordance with that same set of chords for your virtual violin, that piece of software will play along with you with impeccable precision.

The good thing about that virtual violinist is that it does not make a mistake, ever! If you set it to play for an hour straight, it will obey that command tirelessly. Virtual instruments do not need to eat or sleep like human musicians, and even if you want them to, they cannot and will not complain. They will not get in the way of your creative process; they will never argue, and they will obey your instructions to the letter. However you may use them, and regardless of what time of day it is, they are there to address your recording needs.

You can program a virtual instrument to appear as a single musician, and you can make it sound like a dozen musicians are playing all together. We can literally say that with such a computerized accompaniment, the sky is really the limit. On top of it all, a virtual instrument requires no salary. Manpower is greatly diminished, and most importantly, you can save a lot on music production costs because, unlike your former bandmates, computer software does not complain if you get a bigger cut of the allocated talent fee.

Expensive Instruments Become Irrelevant

You hope for the best instruments to be present in your recording sessions because, obviously, you want to attain the best possible sound output. But quality comes at a price, so as you realize there is no way for you, at the moment, to bring high-quality instruments to your home studio, you look for cheaper alternatives and happen to stumble upon a freely downloadable virtual instrument.

After learning it by yourself, you eventually found out that it could really do the trick. It is not as good as the actual thing, but for most listeners, who for the most part are not highly trained musicians, AI-generated accompaniment is actually catchy enough to please them.

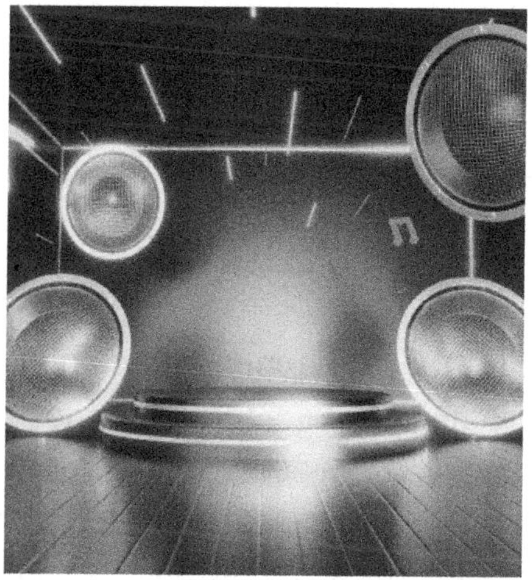

Many music producers, including even the most experienced ones, can truly attest to the fact that there are lots of people that do not really give a damn if it is a real musician playing in the background or if it is just a couple of loops manufactured by computer software (Sgalbazzini, 2021).

There are plenty of high-quality virtual instruments out there that are truly modeled to sound like the most expensive real instruments on the market. As stated previously, there is a virtual instrument for every real one you could think of. The only issue you might face is the amount of time you are willing to invest in looking them up and putting them to the test.

So if you are worried about having to buy real, expensive instruments, try investing plenty of time and little to no money at all, to find the ideal software that can mimic those instruments instead. They are out there waiting for you to try them out—it is just a matter of knowing the sound you want and knowing where to look.

Errors are More Manageable

During those times when analog recording was still the only known method of recording, there were plenty of bands that claimed to have disbanded because of the unimaginable stress that some musicians could not handle. In the higher echelons of the music business, or even in the lower levels where you might belong, there are band leaders and music producers with standards that even the most gifted musicians would have a hard time meeting. As a result, some artists quit halfway through project completion, which led to unwanted court battles and ruined friendships.

As a passionate artist, you hate for that to happen. Thankfully, you have your virtual instruments to help you get the job done—simulations that will never consult a lawyer or sue you in front of a judge. Such a scenario is unlikely because, apart from having no bloated egos that you can hurt, virtual instruments never make mistakes. The only flaws they can generate are those that result from your erroneous instructions. As long as you set the parameters right, they will execute their notes and rhythms in the most precise manner.

Does this mean that virtual instruments can offer the perfection you hope to achieve? Unfortunately, no. The problem with "perfect" is that it is a relative term; it varies from person to person. Your definition of it is not the same as the definition of your best friend, who might also be a music producer like you.

What is great about it, though, is that you can set it to be perfect in your own way, and when it doesn't sound like you want it to, you can easily rectify that with built-in tools, or with the error-fixing plug-ins in your DAW.

Disadvantages of Virtual Instruments

Having grasped the benefits, you might be convinced now that computerized music is something you should use for your benefit. Clearly, they can make almost any imaginable music-producing problem essentially non-existent. In all fairness, though, virtual instruments have some downsides as well. Let us discuss some of their greatest weaknesses.

Talent Degradation

As you may have noticed while studying virtual instruments, the time you spend playing your guitar or any of your preferred instruments has decreased. You hate to admit this, but this is most likely happening to you right now. Naturally, you need to master the ins and outs of your chosen virtual instrument software, and this requires a great deal of time and focus in both physical and mental aspects.

You only have two hands; you cannot possibly tweak your MIDI while using your other limbs as well to play your instruments at exactly the same time. In the process of learning how to program virtual tools, there is an evident downside: your natural talent for playing the instrument you have dearly loved for years has greatly diminished.

This is what those grandpa-level musicians are talking about: musical finesse and the very definition of musical artistry are experiencing an evident demise, and you, as a music producer of the digital age, are offering a helping hand to make it happen. Why? Because you have fallen in love with an AI-driven software tool and are using it to craft your majestic symphonies.

The debate about this issue could go on endlessly, and it would be extremely hard to determine which side would eventually win. However you may put virtual instruments to use, just be certain that even though your talent might degrade at some point, you have to rekindle that old flame you had during those early days when you still loved performing your preferred instrument. Whether you perform in front of huge crowds, or maybe just inside the private space of your own bedroom, virtual instruments must be treated as mere tools—never allow them to replace natural talent.

Poor Emulation of Realistic Sound

When you hear that your favorite band is arriving in town to play live, you'll be very willing to cancel any important appointment just to see them on stage in all their raw glory. Why live shows are still among the most irresistible events that people flock to is because "performance rawness" awaits them.

No matter how many times you hear the recordings of your favorite artists or how many times you have seen them on video, you cannot help but be enthralled when you see them live onstage with your naked eyes. There is really something about seeing them perform their musical craft in the most real and exceptional way they can.

But when using virtual instruments, such a level of reality cannot really be attained, at least for the time being. No matter how brilliantly crafted a virtual instrument might be, nothing of its kind is ever compelling enough to emulate the kind of authenticity that only human musicians can deliver.

Even with virtual drums, the most popular kind of virtual instruments ever, the best ones are still incapable of perfectly mimicking the kind of kicks and grooves of excellent human drummers. For the time being, digital drum beats for the most part are still regarded by experts as very "robotic" in providing percussive rhythms.

But the thing is that most listeners are totally oblivious to this. Most of them would never care if it was a real drummer playing in the background or if it was some programmed software robot. But if you are the kind of music producer who wants to be taken seriously, generating robotic hymns is something you must work very hard to avoid.

Being a marketable music producer includes having a solid portfolio, and being good at working with real instruments is something that the biggest names in the music industry are always on the lookout for. In addition, plenty of high-paying artists still highly prefer those with natural talents. If you are only proficient with virtual instruments, then you might not be someone they are willing to work with.

Real and natural-sounding music must never depart from your artistic expression. No matter how eager you might be to learn modern tools to further your music, you must never ignore the inner urge that nags at you to play your instrument with your hands and limbs from time to time—for the sake of love, for the sake of artistic passion.

Substandard Poetry

Instrumentation has nothing to do with the process of writing lyrics. But since we are discussing the weaknesses of AI in helping us with our music, this next section is something worth mentioning. This might appear very strange to most of us, but some AI tools are actually being used experimentally right now to generate song lyrics.

Google, as one of the biggest names in the software industry, is currently pouring in massive amounts of funding for MusicLM, a song creation tool that its creators hope will one day be capable of generating hit songs with AI as its songwriter (Raieli, 2023). Nobody can really tell yet if this will turn out to be a success, but for the time being, AI cannot create compelling lyrics just yet.

AI is quite good in terms of accuracy and in generating captivating chord patterns that can easily get people hooked. But in terms of generating lyrics that can capture people's emotions, it is still very mediocre at best.

This should help us understand that in using AI to artistically craft our music, we must accept some harsh truths—there are aspects of it that we cannot utilize just yet, at least for the moment. Since AI is unquestionably good at creating perfect rhythms and catchy hooks, it should be best employed in such categories.

In your hopes of captivating your listeners at a more emotional level, or in generating the poetry you hope the audience will fall in love with, trusting your own vocabulary is still the best approach. For now, AI is a bad poet; you just have to accept this undeniable limitation.

AI is most useful in replicating elements, reducing manpower, and cutting costs. In emulating the "human touch" of music though, it is still not as powerful as you might have expected. In using virtual tools in producing your music, you must be very careful in balancing AI and human intelligence. Not heeding this would be a mistake if you are hoping to carve a niche in the very competitive avenue of the music industry.

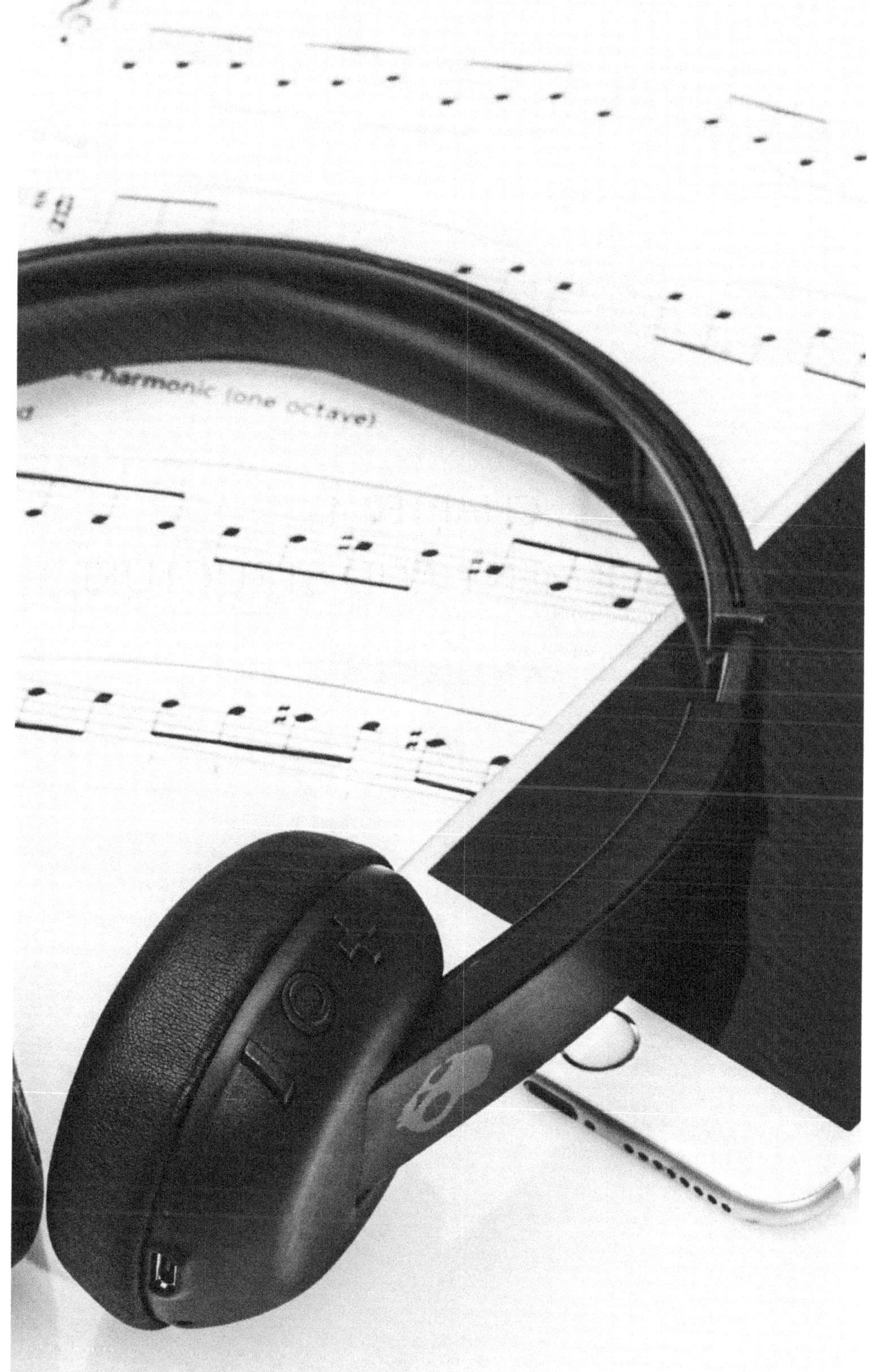
harmonic (one octave)

CHAPTER 4
ARRANGEMENT AND STRUCTURE

With what we've learned so far about track recording and virtual instruments, it should be safe to admit that songwriting can be much easier than it used to be. No computer software can help us acquire the natural talents that the most gifted songwriters possess, but anyone can see that technology can greatly enhance the songwriting abilities we already have.

All songs, no matter how brilliantly crafted they might be, would not sound good if they were not arranged well. Furthermore, they must be structured based on the current technical requirements of the music industry.

There is no doubt that a naturally talented songwriter can create majestic tunes and melodies. But without the finishing touches and polishing abilities of audio experts, their songs would not become as lovely and polished as they appear to the listening public.

Behind the recording process of every hit song you love are the arranging and structuring methods of audio experts and record producers. We'll assume that, as a novice in this field, you are serving such roles in the recording process of your own songs.

What you will learn here are the drills you have to undergo after recording all the sound elements your song may contain. While this does not guarantee that you will become a hitmaker, it will certainly go a long way toward establishing your reputation as a great music producer in the long run.

Securing and Preparing Your Tracks

Like a good soldier who makes sure that his weapons will function appropriately in battle, you should make sure that the components of your musical piece are very well-organized. The objective is to accomplish the mission in the most efficient way possible.

It is understandable that you are fired up to start mixing right away. But before you get to that intricate process, there are necessary preparations and precautionary measures you have to go through. As the mixing process gets more complicated, you'll want to avoid confusion and frustration by putting your recorded tracks in the best order you can.

Preparing and organizing your tracks should happen under the assumption that you have already recorded all the vocal parts, as well as the instrumentation parts. It also has to be assumed that you recorded them based on the principles established in Chapter 2.

Even though we are not yet officially in the mixing process, you are now prompted to load all your tracks into your DAW's workspace area so you can work on editing each one of them later. Before you actually import them to your DAW, make sure that you have already given them distinctive file names so you can identify them easily.

Another vital task at this point would be creating backups of all your tracks. Whether you are a newbie or a pro, backing up your tracks is a strict protocol you must follow because there is a huge possibility that your files could get corrupted or get accidentally damaged while mixing and editing them.

The good thing about most DAWs, though, is that they have their own backup prompts that will remind you to read from the source file or make a copy of it. But even the best DAWs can crash from time to time, so you have to make it a habit to always make backups of your tracks. It is better to be safe now than be teary-sorry later.

Arranging and Labeling Tracks Properly

This is where you should start importing all your tracks to your DAW. Once all of them are loaded into the workspace, you need to arrange them accordingly. The most recommended order would be to have the drum parts in the topmost area, followed by the bass parts, the rhythm guitar, and all the other instruments that comprise the rhythm section of your song.

Similar to what is recommended during recording, the drums need to be positioned first before the other tracks. It should be on the topmost part of the workspace because you need to be sure that all the other parts are synced to its beats. As you load each track after the drum parts, you need to listen to each one to make sure they are truly following the "heartbeat of the song."

This step is extremely important, since keeping your tracks neatly synced is a must in music production. Proper timing is vital in every recording session, and if it is not properly observed, your song will not be as polished as you hoped.

If you recorded your tracks using a metronome or a drum machine and have checked them to be precisely synced with the fixed tempo, then there is no need to worry. They will surely be in perfect rhythm with the entire flow of the song. If the sync is out, which is almost always the case, you will need to synchronize your tracks carefully to match the rhythm section. This can be very time-consuming, but is essential to produce a good mix. Every good DAW will have appropriate tools to allow you to precisely synchronize the instrumental and vocal parts.

Since the number of tracks or layers visible on your DAW would be dependent on what type of song it is and how many instruments or vocals are included, it should be up to you which track is placed in a specific area of your workspace. There is no solid rule as to which track should be on top or which one should be on the bottom. The whole point of this is to make sure that you will find it a lot easier to sync and arrange your tracks while mixing.

Labeling and Color Coding

For added convenience, you should label each track and even each section of the track for complex recordings. For instance, you might want to put labels such as "intro, verse, chorus, etc." While this is not really necessary if you are working on an acoustic track with one singer, it is a must when you are mixing a multi-track song played by a full band.

Labeling provides the convenience of pinpointing which part needs to be dealt with as you go along in the process. While looking at your tracks' waveforms for hours, you could start seeing things that are not really there, which could lead to plenty of headaches as the process dragged on further. As someone who is just starting out, you have to instill in yourself the habit of being organized—this will pave the way for a high level of efficiency.

Writing notes is also worth considering. Most DAWs are equipped with a notepad where you can type track descriptions. This is particularly helpful when working with other sound editors, since they will not need to listen to entire tracks just to find out what they are dealing with.

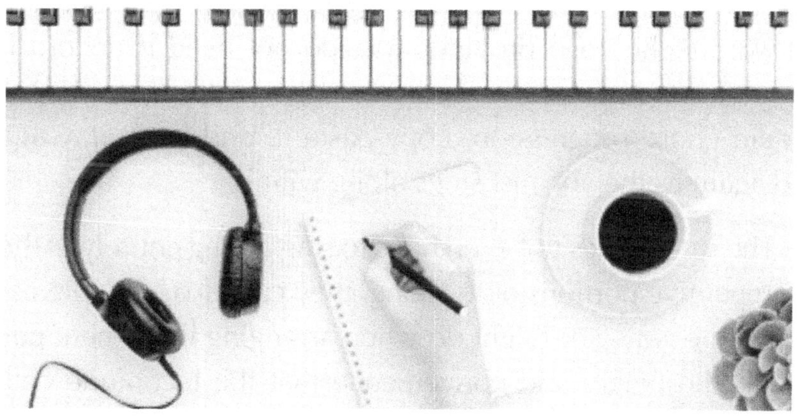

Some DAWs also enable you to embed color codes into your tracks or the portions that comprise them. Instead of labeling portions as "verse, chorus, ad lib, etc.," you could apply color coding instead so they could be easily located as you zoom in or out within your workspace.

There are plenty of tips and tricks in preparing your tracks. Feel free to create your own method. The point of this is to keep you organized. You have to find a way to lay out your tracks in such a way that the least confusion will take place later on. Yes, a great deal of confusion could arise, especially if you work with your tracks for many hours—you have to be patient enough to handle this.

Working With Loops and Samples

In the days of analog recording, vocals and instruments were mostly recorded in full takes. A singer would sing a song in its entirety, including repeating the same choruses or redundant verses in every take. Instrumentalists would also undergo the same routine, which was undoubtedly very burdensome for everyone.

But thankfully for us, such a regimen is now just a part of history. Today, we have the unparalleled convenience that software technology provides. We do not need to record full takes of song parts anymore. All we have to do is record a certain chord progression, copy-paste it, and let it play again and again as the vocalist sings along with it.

The singer does not even have to sing a song entirely. If there are repetitive portions of the song, they can also be copied and pasted the way you might do when arranging instrument parts. This is the magic and convenience that the technique called "looping and sampling" offers.

As you have learned about MIDI, even non-musicians can already make very compelling music pieces. If you are already a talented musician, you can make your tasks so much easier and less laborious as well. Instead of recording all the strums and riffs of your guitar parts throughout your song's duration, you just have to record a superb take and copy-paste them whenever necessary.

Some musicians still insist on playing the full song, and when you work with such people, you can certainly allow them to play a song all the way through. While editing their music later, you have to exercise your rights in choosing which parts sound the best.

Once you have identified the best instrument loops from the entire take, you may then isolate and replicate them until a full track of intertwined loops is fully assembled. Once you mix it with all the other tracks smoothly, people will not care anymore how it was recorded. The objective is to come up with a flawless output, and if software technology helps us get the job done, we can certainly utilize it to our advantage.

While traditional musicians may nag at you for this, you should find great comfort in the idea that there is no way for most of the listening public to find out—unless you decide to tell them. Obviously, this seems like a means of cheating. But then, technology is available for us to use to bring about a great level of ease to our very complex job. It is not a crime to use digitization to "cheat" our way to finish things up faster while bringing our music to the level of perfection that we highly desire.

Creating Uniqueness and Variety: Using Auto-Tune and Pitch Correction

Embellishing elements that can make our music more interesting is something we always think of. Since we already acknowledged that there is no harm in utilizing technology to

make our job easier, how about we use it a bit further to make our music more interesting? How about we make alternate versions of our songs by toying around with the tools that your DAW provides?

In this section, let us discuss even more tools and features that you might initially hate. As you get used to the convenience they offer, though, you might begin to understand that when used sparingly, they can be truly helpful in making your digital music production endeavors much more convenient.

If you have been religiously studying digital music production, you might have heard music traditionalists complain about the existence of "the evil auto-tune." Yes, we already established the notion that digitization has made musicians lazy and has degraded their talents to the lowest imaginable levels. But before you totally side with the traditionalists and begin hating digital music, you might want to hear the benefits that auto-tuning can offer first.

For one, it can save time and even provide you with extra moments with a singer even if they are no longer present. Obviously, you cannot ask the singers to repeat the recording in their absence. You can, however, correct pitch errors by adjusting some of the misplaced pitches in the melody. As long as that singer is capable of performing good quality vocals the way you wanted in rehearsal, the audience should not have any problem with it once you've got it tuned and synched.

Another benefit that auto-tune offers is that it can add more variety and flavor to your song. When used creatively, it can bring about a unique projection out of a singer's natural voice. Though it is deemed a wicked tool by some, it can also serve as an avenue for success for some artists.

Playboi Carti, Lil Uzi Vert, Travis Scott, and T-Pain are among those who have achieved global popularity because of auto-tune. You might have also heard Cher's "Believe" in which a unique kind of vocal inflection is rendered (Madden, 2019).

Auto-tuning is not only applicable to vocals; it is also used by instrumentalists to make sure that their instruments are perfectly in tune in cases where they failed to notice that their instruments were not tuned properly during a live performance.

Antares, Celemony Melodyne, and Synchro Arts Revoice are among the most widely used auto-tune software applications. They do not come cheap, though, as this type of software goes for between $100 and $1000, while some are available on a subscription basis. There are also those that you can download for free. You just have to expect that the outputs from such software will sound very dull and robotic.

Whether you decide to use auto-tune is a matter of personal preference. It is included in this discussion because we are finding ways to make our music production tasks much easier. This is just another tool to bring variety to the music we hope will gain attention.

Structuring and arranging your songs can be very challenging and painstaking. One tool might be better than another, while some tools might be "evil" from the perspective of others. Regardless of how you absorb those ideas, stay focused on your own objectives.

Never let anyone's opinions drown your own. If there are tools that can ease up the burden, then you must stop listening to arguments and decide on what gets the job done in the most convenient and most satisfying manner.

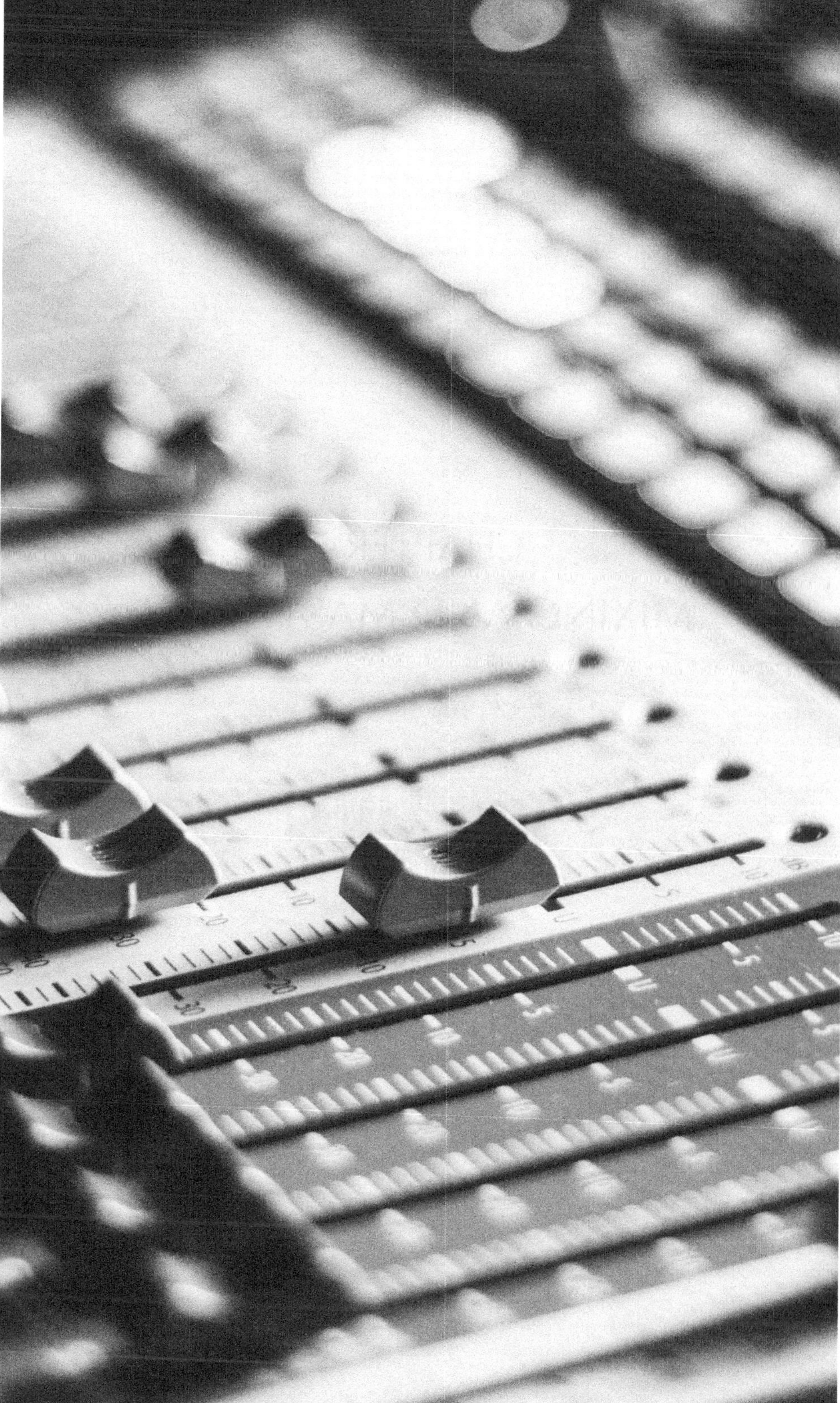

CHAPTER 5
MIXING AND MASTERING

Like a cinematographer who expects scenes to be as emotionally and visually captivating as possible, proficient music producers expect their finished recordings to be mesmerizing and enthralling in every possible way.

It is not enough that the vocals and instruments are laid out in such a manner that they hit the time signature right and that they are aligned melodically—they have to be mixed strategically. They must not only sound right, but they also have to sound "addictively beautiful" as well.

Mixing and mastering may appear basically the same, but for every experienced music producer out there, they are different fields of discipline (Dixon, 2019). They must work hand-in-hand though, because one cannot totally materialize without the other. Let us discuss the steps you will undergo in the mixing process of your tracks, which will eventually become the hit song you have been dreaming would hit the airwaves.

Before we actually begin, you have to bear in mind that the next steps are presented in a very simplified form. This means that the following is designed to be applicable regardless of what DAW you are using or what kind of song you are mixing. By proceeding, it is assumed that you have already arranged your tracks as discussed in the previous chapter.

Many sound engineers would have their own list of steps. Some would exaggerate the process that it would take to become a professional sound engineer and make it difficult to understand what they really mean. We will not do that here. This is meant to be understood by a newbie, so our discussion will be as basic and condensed as possible, while still being very comprehensive from a layman's perspective.

Crucial Mixing Steps

Cleanup and Noise Removal

Most experts skip the "cleanup" part and even refuse to count it as part of the process. The reason is that most of them have very highly-trained ears, so all the unwanted noises or frequencies that might appear in the recordings will just vanish as they go along with their usual mixing routine. However, as a novice, it is highly recommended that you do some cleanup with your tracks before proceeding further.

It is called "cleanup" because literally, you will be cleaning your tracks of that unwanted background noise that will make your output extremely muddy over time. Noise removal is one of the most basic routines you have to do as you embark on your first steps as a home-based music producer.

We have to assume that during your first recording attempts, you are using low-cost equipment. You are most likely on a tight budget, so you bought the most affordable music gear available. The most obvious problem with such devices is that your recording output will not be as naturally crisp and clean as what you would have when recording with expensive ones.

There is no need to worry, though, because your chosen DAW

can still remove most of those undesirable background noises that might be present while recording. We have to be clear, though, that the kind of noise we are talking about here is "white noise," which comes from your ventilators and the humming of the electronic equipment you have in the room.

If you followed the tips in Chapter 2, then you should have understood by now that there are certain kinds of noise that are impossible to remove with the tools of your DAW. Using the noise removal feature of your DAW is typically done by highlighting a sample of the noise you want to get rid of. The best way to identify this would be to select the first few seconds of background silence at the beginning of your track.

Once the software identifies this as the kind of noise you want to remove, it will work its way throughout the entire length of your track and remove it. You may do it more than once for each of your tracks, depending on how noisy they are. The more you do, the lower quality your end mix will be, so it's always best to start as clean as possible in the recording session.

Compression and Normalization

In addition to removing unwanted noises, you need to make your tracks sound more even and consistent; this is where a process called compression comes into play. It is one of the most important processes during the mixing process because it makes the soft parts of your tracks appear louder while making the louder parts a bit softer.

Vocals are usually the most tweaked tracks during the compression phase of mixing music. This is to even out high peaks and low valleys in the amplitude in order to make it more consistent and go harmoniously with the other instruments. Because MIDI tracks appear more consistent than real instruments that are recorded manually, they should not require any post compression. The most typical settings you might see in your DAW's compressor would be threshold, noise floor, ratio, and attack/release time. To make your tracks as natural sounding as possible, you must not stray too far from the following settings:

- Threshold : -12 db
- Noise floor : -40 db
- Ratio : 2:1
- Attack time : 0.2 secs
- Release time : 1.0 sec

You can play around with these settings until you get your desired results. With most tracks, though, these numbers should be enough to make the softest parts of a track already discernible. Straying too far from these settings would make your track, especially if it is a vocal track, sound very weird. Unless weirdness is required in your mix, it is strongly recommended that you stick to that given configuration or choose one that does not stretch too far from it (Buzzsprout, 2022).

By selecting the entire track and applying the default compression settings of your DAW, the track will have a significant transformation, in the sense that the highs and lows of its volume will become much more even.

Next to compression, normalization must also happen. This is to ensure that no clipping happens to a particular track as it is played. Clipping is a mixing term applied to the distortion that happens when the volume level goes above zero dB. Sound engineers recommend that sound outputs should be within -3 or lower to prevent music from sounding poorly (Audiosorcerer, 2022).

While mixing, you should look at the playback meter of your DAW regularly. If it becomes red, it means the audio being played is clipping. It should be avoided because it could also potentially damage the speakers when played repeatedly. This problem can be easily solved by using the normalize tool in your DAW's menu.

Each and every track must be compressed and normalized to ensure output quality. For every compression you do, normalization should happen right after so that the likelihood of clipping is minimized.

EQ and Panning

To enhance the sound quality even further, a process called equalization must also take place. It can be defined in simple terms as the process of amplitude adjustment of sound frequencies to attain the clearest sound output possible. As explained in Chapter 2, the basic science behind sound is that it travels in waves. It could be at a

high frequency, a low frequency, or somewhere in the middle (Science Learning Hub, 2019).

To make a track sound much clearer, the high-pitch amplitude levels of it could be boosted to make it sharper, or if you want to have a stronger kick to your beats, the low-pitch amplitude levels of it could be enhanced. Getting too deep into the science behind this would be overwhelming, so let us simplify it.

The most common element you need to understand in equalization is the balance between bass and treble. Let us just say that bass is that low-pitched tone you hear in a music track. Conversely, the high-pitched tones you hear are called treble. Now, to make an instrument sound better, you have to adjust the bass and treble levels appropriately to make the sound of your overall mix sound a lot better.

But as a beginner, how would you know if a certain bass or treble level is acceptable or not, compared to the industry standards? The simplest solution for this is to use the EQ presets in your chosen DAW. It will be equipped with settings given by the software manufacturer. You should utilize them as a beginner first, then develop your own settings as you gain experience.

In working with stereo sound, a technique called panning is also employed. This is the process of manipulating the left and right channels of your tracks, so they would only appear on just one channel or in both channels. Many audio technicians use this technique to solve the problem of muddy mixes.

For instance, the muted sound of a guitar could be played on the right channel only, while some minor percussion could be played only on the left channel. By preventing a multitude of tracks from coming out of the same speaker all at once, a much clearer mix can be attained.

Volume Balancing

Not to be confused with equalizing, this phase is about simply increasing or decreasing the volumes of each of your tracks. While this is just about turning levels up or down, this is one of the trickiest tasks you need to go through since you will have to get back to this phase again and again throughout the entire mixing process.

While working with a particular setting or sound effect, you might find that one track appears very indiscernible to your ears compared to the others. To prevent it from getting buried in the volume of the other tracks, you have to go back and tweak it to a much better level.

While doing that, you might find that another track is overshadowed by the volume of the most recent one you worked on. This drill could get really painstaking at times, so taking a break would be ideal after working for many hours. After giving your eyes and ears some rest, you may then go back to adjusting the volume levels of your tracks so they can be heard much clearer.

This is a skill that takes a considerable amount of time to master. As a newbie, you might find this rather exhausting because some audio sequences could sound the same to your ears. From time to time, you have to remind yourself to take a break to prevent burnouts that could lead to ugly results. Artistry must be a priority, so resting a bit is one of the important tips you have to bear in mind.

Space and Effects

Regardless of the type of music you are working on, adding

effects to your tracks is part of the process. Some effects are very obvious, while others are so subtle that they are almost non-existent. In both the vocal and instrumental parts of your songs, certain audio configurations must be done so that even the most natural voices that require almost no correction can be enhanced even further.

Putting some "sense of space" or reverb into your tracks is a trick you can use to make the vocals or the instrument sound bigger or fuller than they actually are. For instance, you could make the drummer sound like he is playing from a distance, or you could make the guitarist sound like he is sitting right next to you as he strums the strings.

This is a reverb element called "room size," and it is one of the most common settings that audio technicians work on a lot while enhancing an audio track. A larger room setting means the instruments appear to be played in a huge area. Conversely, setting it lower means they are played in a much smaller room.

Other vital reverb elements include damping, pre-delay, and reverberance. The simplest way to understand them is by singing in a bathroom. You'll notice that reflected sound as you sing or speak there. Reverb settings are very helpful if you can embed them strategically in your tracks. It makes vocals and instruments sound more professional, in addition to making them sound much fuller.

In setting the room sizes of your tracks, you should make sure that none of them are exactly at the same level. This is a helpful tip, especially when there are plenty of instruments in your mix. If the room size of your drums is 60%, your lead guitar should be somewhere between 20% and 30%. The reverb of your bass guitar and rhythm guitar should be somewhere close to the same room size as your drums because they are also rhythmic instruments.

The room size of your vocals is something you have to decide for yourself, or it may depend on the singer's preference. There is no strict rule for this. The consensus is that, as long as each and every instrument can be heard properly, you are heading in the right direction.

Aside from reverb, there are plenty of extra effects you might want to use including echoes, delays, cross-fades, pitch shifts, and others. Implementing them should be done according to your discretion. The most important tip to remember is that you must "never overdo nor overuse" them.

The audience in general will be much more appreciative if what they hear is very natural. The more effects they can hear from your output, the more they might think that you are not that talented a musician.

Unless the artist you are working with specifically dictates that a certain sound effect must be applied, you should usually avoid any overpowering effects. Real beauty lies in simplicity, and in the act of music mixing, this principle is highly applicable.

To simplify the process of using these audio effects, you should tend to resort to using presets. In any DAW you may consider using, there are plenty of predefined settings designed by expert audio engineers that come along with it.

By simply clicking and applying them, your tracks would sound very similar to those that we can classify as "industry standards." Using them will go a long way toward making your tracks sound "good enough." If they do not, you have to give them some minor adjustments until they sound ideal enough for your tastes.

Re-checking and Exporting

Once you have applied the above-mentioned steps to all of your tracks, it is highly recommended that you stand back and let them all play together. If you have been working with your headphones, it is always best to hear your mix from a large speaker as you decide on adding more texture to your music.

Most audio engineers would recommend this because, after many hours of hearing it from your headphones, there might be some levels and frequencies that appear a bit different once heard from a different output device (Fox, 2023).

You have to listen to your mixed tracks again and again to make sure that each one of them is at an ideal level and that none of them are buried in the mix. If you are not satisfied yet with the loudness or softness of some portions of your tracks, you have to go back to any of the above steps.

You should make only minor adjustments each time to make sure that the real settings that you find most pleasant will not be ruined. One of the best techniques for this is to save different versions of your project with different filenames. You might want to name it "experimental output" so that the good mix that you decide as your best one will not be destroyed through intensive experimentation.

If you are confident that the sound you are hearing is what you were hoping to achieve, it should be time to export your tracks all together as a single music track. It could be done with just a click of a button, which would prompt you to input track details such as song title, album title, artist name, and other relevant details.

The final file could be MP3, WAV, or any of the other music file types mentioned in the previous chapters. Since you understand already that WAV is the highest fidelity type, you should always export your final audio output in that format.

You have to acknowledge that as you listen to your final output over the next few hours or days, you could have some bursts of artistry that dictate some changes or final touches. As you do so, you have to heed what Leonardo da Vinci once said, "Art is never finished, only abandoned." You have to embrace the idea that even though your song appears perfect to you, you still have to be open to further improvements.

Mastering Guidelines

By now, you have probably listened to your finished output dozens of times already, gone through your mix repeatedly, and made extra tweaks to enhance it a bit further. Now you feel like your song is really perfect and ready to be sent out into the world so that the audience and your potential fans will include it in their playlists along with the other artists they adore so much.

You might think your song is ready, but you have to think again. In the creation of an album, or even in the production of just a single song, there is one final process that needs to happen—a mastering process that ensures your musical output meets the quality standards of the music industry.

Mastering is mainly about importing the final track of your song back into your DAW and making additional tweaks to its EQ settings. This is to ensure that listeners hear what is meant to be heard and that no unwanted sound elements are emanating from the speakers as your song is played.

The difference between mixing and mastering is that the former lets you work with multiple tracks, while the latter is only about fixing whatever irregularities are present in the final single track. As you tweak your EQ to adjust all the frequencies to make it better, here are the guidelines you must bear in mind to ensure that the mastering process truly serves its purpose.

Vocal Inflections are Clear Enough

Regardless of the genre your music belongs to, the vocals must stand out compared to all the other tracks. Sure, there are parts when one instrument needs to be louder than the others, but for the most part, the words that come out of the singer's mouth must be very clear. Otherwise, what is the point of writing a song in the first place?

One of the strongest reasons why a song becomes so popular is because of the message it conveys. So if the vocal inflections are not that clear, it means your mix is not polished enough. In addition to the compression process that your vocal track went through, the ideal balance of treble and bass must also be executed to give it the fullness or sharpness it is meant to project.

As you go about your mastering process, you have to work on tweaking the frequencies of the vocals first before fine-tuning everything else. There is a reason why the vocalist is called the front man, and in the final form of your song, the vocals and nothing else must stand out from the rest.

All Instruments Can Be Heard Clearly

This is the main reason why volume balancing is one of the trickiest tasks in the mixing process. Turning levels up and down can be very frustrating because, although some instruments already appear very thin in the mix, they could still sound louder than the other tracks.

In the mastering process, you need to carefully identify which tracks need to be the loudest or the softest in a particular portion of a song. When a guitar solo takes place, you might need to tone the other frequencies down so they will not overshadow that solo. When another instrument is meant to stand out, you might want to decrease the intensity of the others too.

When all instruments are playing together, you need to ensure that all of them can be really perceived by the listeners' ears. If one instrument appears missing, then there is something wrong with your mix, so you have to tweak it with your EQ during mastering to make its presence more noticeable. If this doesn't do the job, you'll have to go back and re-mix the tracks properly.

It Sounds Good in All Kinds of Speakers

This is where you should be reminded that when mixing, you need to listen to your work with your headphones and also from a pair of large speakers. You should also try to listen to your song from within the room as well as outside of it, if possible.

You might also want to try listening at the highest volume possible while standing outside the building. The mysterious thing about mixing music is that there are certain subtleties and nuances that are not really there while you are sitting in front of your computer and staring at your work.

But when you are away from your screen, there are sound elements you might hear that you never expected to emerge. This is one of the most significant dilemmas suffered by even the most experienced audio engineers. You have to learn to adapt to this.

In addition, you have to let your song play through the speakers of mobile devices such as tablets, laptops, and smartphones. You have to acknowledge that the great majority of your audience will most likely listen to your song on their phones. If your song does not sound good on handheld gadgets, then we have to say that the music you make is not in ideal shape.

To prevent this from happening, you have to practice this drill right during the mixing process itself. As you take breaks, you have to observe your mix using various headphones, average-sized speakers, and those oversized sound systems used in concerts if you have them accessible. This is to ensure that during the mastering process, they contain the musical elements needed to make them sound good in all kinds of speakers.

It Sounds Presentable When Played With Other Songs

"Everybody fails the first time," so the saying goes. No matter how nicely you have done your mix, it might still be sub-par compared to the popular ones that are already out there on the market. As a novice, there is nothing wrong with failing during your first attempt, or even in the ones that come after it.

As long as you took all the previous lessons seriously, your mastering regimen should still be able to ensure that with a few more tweaks, your song would sound as good, or at least appear to be near the level of the songs you consider to be the best.

The most ideal method of accomplishing this is by making a playlist of some songs that would serve as comparable outputs to your final track. Include your output there, and listen to the entire playlist to see how different or similar it is next to the others. You might then want to go back to mastering it until you achieve the "totally polished output" you truly hoped for.

In any case, if you are not satisfied with your final mastered track and you feel you could have done better, then by all means, you should get back to the mixing process. As a newbie, you are entitled to a much longer deadline, and to be honest, there is no real "deadline" while you are still in the learning phase as a music producer.

Sound Polishing Tips

While you are in the process of mixing or mastering, you might want to consider applying these extra tips for achieving a polished, professional sound.

Cutting Instead of Boosting

The most basic approach to enhancing a track's audio would be to boost its volume. The problem with doing this too much is that it could make your mix even muddier. An alternative remedy that could lead to the same outcome would be cutting other tracks instead of boosting the one you want to stand out.

This could make the overall outcome of the entire mix much cleaner because the tracks would not sound like they are trying to trample over each other while trying to stand out. You have to remember that the real beauty of a song lies in the tracks being laid out harmoniously together.

De-essing

While enhancing the clarity of a vocal track, you might begin to observe that the syllables that contain "S" or "SH" become overly evident. This is called "sibilance," and it is one of the most recurring issues when trying to make a good blend of vocals and instrumentation.

You could solve this by tweaking the 5–10 kHz frequency range of your vocal track in the EQ (Sweetwater, 1997). In mastering, you must never touch any frequencies outside of it because you might damage the other frequencies of the other instruments. For a much easier de-essing process, you could use a de-esser plug-in instead. This could be downloaded for free or obtained as an add-on to your chosen DAW.

Layering

As a newbie, you might find it hard to distinguish subtle configuration changes, especially if you work for too many hours. To make it easier for you, you might consider using the layering technique. Used by even the most experienced sound engineers out there, it is about putting identical tracks together while embedding different settings for each of them.

In your vocals, for instance, you might want to have two or more tracks with different levels of reverb, bass, and treble. One track should serve as your main track, and it must be plain, raw, and sharp. The others would then contain the bass or reverb effects. This gives you a nice chorus effect.

As you play them together, you might want to adjust their volume settings until you get the results you desire. Though layering is highly applicable to vocals, there is no strict rule that prohibits you from applying it to the instruments as well. You should definitely give it a try.

Soft-clipping

Though clipping is something to always avoid at the recording stage, there is a kind of clipping that you could try in the final output of your track. Soft-clipping as it is called, is a kind of distortion found in some analog sound systems. This technique is used by some sound engineers to cater to the "loudness wars" that seem to be very evident in today's music scene. It essentially raises the overall volume of the mix without introducing new peaks or clipping.

As early as the 1940s, there have been some observations that songs that are not loud enough are often ignored by listeners (Clark, 2019). To cater to this, audio engineers came up with soft-clipping to greatly raise audio levels without compromising too much on quality. Like de-essing, soft-clipping can be easily attained using DAW plug-ins. If you are worried that your final track is not as loud as the hit songs you adore, you have to try it out as well.

As you attain expertise in both mixing and mastering, some musicians will hire you to enhance each track that comprises their songs. You could also be hired to master the final track so you can make it ready for the listeners. Regardless of what task they might commission you to do, you have to be ready for both.

This chapter is the highlight of this book, in the sense that it is the most technical and laborious lesson. It is highly recommended that you regularly revisit and redo the drills from time to time until your mixing and mastering skills have reached a satisfactory level..

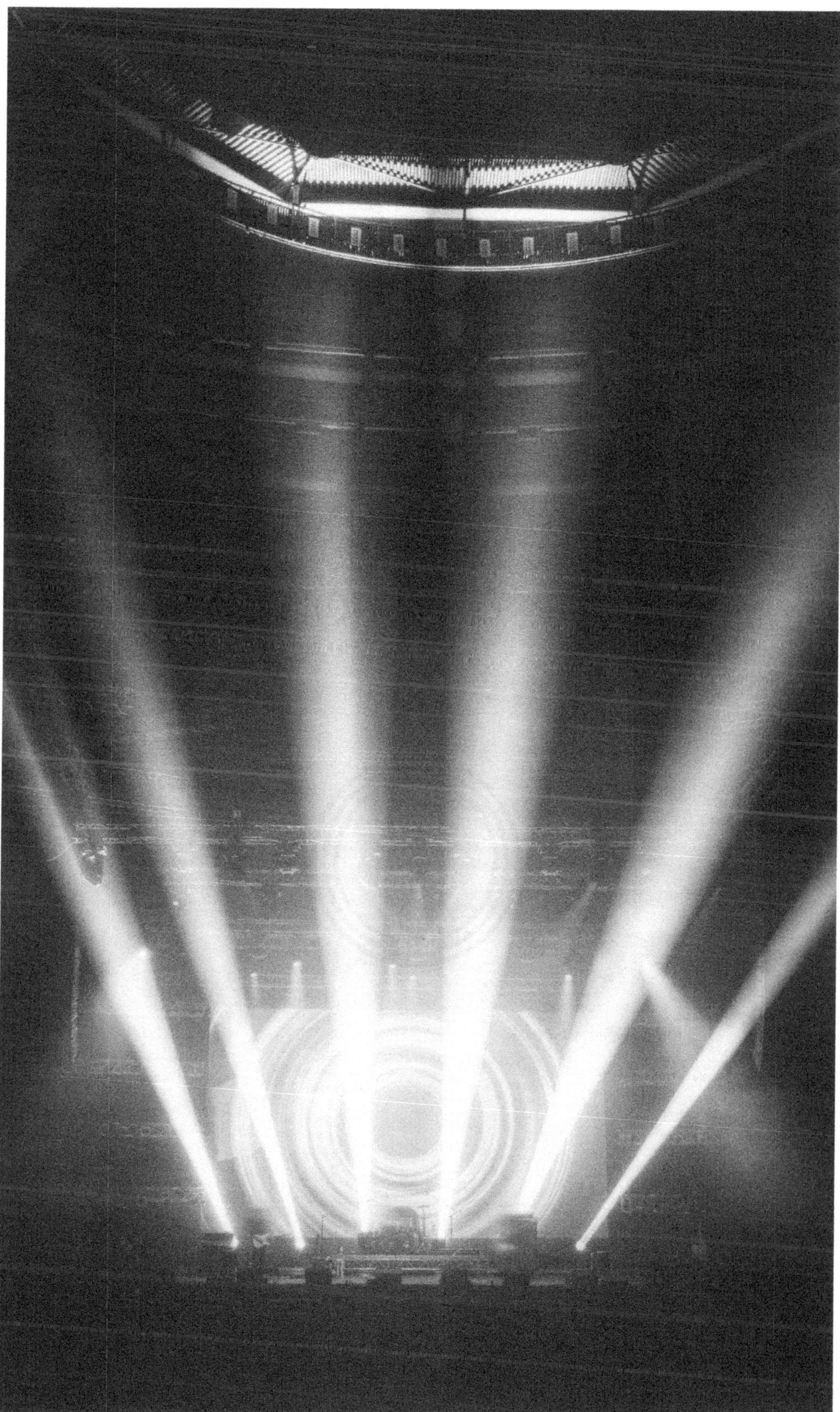

CHAPTER 6
COLLABORATION AND PROMOTION

So, you've written some captivating songs, recorded them, and polished them to perfection. Congratulations! You may think your work is done—you may think that would be the end of it. If that is what you have in mind, then you are greatly mistaken. The process of producing music and making a desirable recording out of it is just one facet of a very huge process—it is just a single cog in a complex, huge piece of machinery that you chose to be a part of.

There is yet another vital element that you need to integrate, an element that is just as intricate and painstaking as the procedures you went through while recording and refining those lovely songs you wrote. This element is called music promotion, and it includes learning how to do the math and how to come up with the right strategies so that people will not ignore the symphonies you wrote. They have to take heed, listen, and digest the artistic product that you worked so hard for!

If you have been passionate about becoming a hitmaker these past few years, chances are you have already grasped that the music industry is not the same as it was a few decades ago. The methods of music promotion and distribution have significantly changed. You have to learn how modern music is published in the digital age. If you refuse to adapt to such changes, your fantasy of becoming the next best-selling hitmaker will remain as it is—a fantasy.

Digitization might have paved the way for great financial losses from the viewpoint of multi-million record labels. Fortunately for the likes of you, digital technology is here to save the day, and it is the ultimate hero that might make you truly profitable as an independent, DIY musician or record producer.

How and Where Should You Distribute Your Music?

To earn a living out of music is every musician's dream. While owning a mansion with a garage filled with expensive sports cars might be too far-fetched, utilizing your music to pay the bills would appear more realistic. The thing is, it is not too impossible either—as long as you distribute your music on the right platforms.

So where can you find the right platforms? And most importantly, how can you find the ideal one that will serve as the perfect fit for the music career you're aiming for? That platform is something that you hope will bring in monetary gain that will change your life, from a financial standpoint, so to speak. Choosing that platform needs to be done right, and this is where some in-depth research should come into play.

Gone are the days when people went to music stores and bought cassette tapes, vinyl, and CDs. It should follow without question that releasing your music in these mediums is totally impractical, not to mention, totally unwise. Some pop stars still sell their records this way, though. But unless you've already attained the level of stardom that Ed Sheeran or Taylor Swift have, you must never think of releasing your album in any of those physical formats.

So how should you release your music then? To answer that directly, digital platforms are the best portals to tap into. These days, they are the best and only option that an aspiring pop star like you should definitely pick. Are they easily accessible? Yes. Do they have standards that must be strictly followed? Technically, yes. Are they expensive? Surprisingly, no.

Choosing Your Platform and Distributor

To release your music digitally, you need to weigh your options carefully so you can pick the right platform or the right distributor. As you do so, you have to ask yourself, Would I want my music to be presented in sound format alone? Or would I want to make video performances as well?

Since answering the second question would entail a whole new level of difficulty, you would most certainly choose the direction of the first question. Having said that, releasing your songs through audio streaming platforms should be the first viable option a novice music artist like you should strongly consider.

You have already been through the meticulous process of recording and mastering your songs. This means that you are only a few steps away from releasing it into cyberspace, so people can consume it. As your career begins to climb and as you earn some decent income out of it, you might then consider releasing your music in video format, which is a massive separate lesson in itself that must be studied at another time.

Now back to the main topic at hand, which is choosing your online platform and distributor. For sure, you're aiming for the best option there is, and if we were to ask the most profitable online musicians, they would answer without any hesitation that the best platform where you could release your music and make money online is none other than Spotify.

Other equally good options include Soundcloud, Pandora, and Deezer. But since you're most likely aiming for the best possible platform where you could be heard with the widest reach, Spotify should be the very first direction to head in (Pendlebury, 2022).

One thing you have to be aware of, though, is that, unlike YouTube, where you can just upload content after signing up, you can't directly do that in Spotify. First, you need to pick a distributor, sign up for it, pay some fees, and your music is released to dozens of online music stores on the web. Yes, you read that right—dozens!

The most recommended distributors out there that could scatter your album to plenty of online stores include DistroKid, TuneCore, Stem, and AWAL. As of this writing, DistroKid appears to be the best for most online musicians and indie artists. For as little as $20, you can upload an unlimited number of songs for an entire year.

Apart from providing additional services that include improving the volume settings of your tracks to ideal levels, it also distributes your music to 150 online stores. Collecting earnings from all of those stores, and apportioning it to your bandmates and collaborators, are all handled by DistroKid, because of that $20 you paid (Deviant Noise, 2023). That is certainly an offer you could not refuse.

Social Media and Online Communities: The Newest Frontier For Music Promotion

Finding out that online distributors come very cheap might be

a huge relief for you, but there is one sad truth you need to know: the likes of DistroKid and Tunecore are not responsible for promoting your music. This means that just because they released your music on Spotify, Amazon, and Apple Music, it is not a guarantee that millions of listeners will follow your music and worship you like you're some kind of divine musical being.

Releasing your music is one thing; promoting it, however, is another story. You still need to do much harder work, and that includes reaching out to people through virtual avenues where they usually flock together. And if we were to ask around, there is no better place to promote your musical artistry than within the realms of social networking sites.

Social media is both an irresistible and unstoppable force—you cannot ignore it, and you cannot avoid it. Facebook, Twitter, Instagram, and a bunch of other similar platforms (many of which you likely haven't even heard of yet), are here to stay. Most probably, their omniscience will still be very prevalent in the next few decades, because even your kids or grandkids, and perhaps you yourself, have had a hard time ignoring the addiction it inflicted on humanity.

Since social media is the ultimate digital hangout for people of all ages in this generation, it would be utterly unwise to not promote your music on Facebook and the like. Thankfully, Facebook advertising is surprisingly cheap—even the most impoverished musicians can certainly afford it.

For as little as $1 a day, you could launch an ad campaign that could reach a few thousand viewers, provided, of course, that the ad you crafted is attractive enough (Paquette, 2020). On YouTube, you could also follow a similar approach with nearly the same amount.

There are other similar platforms out there that can provide you with endless promotional possibilities. But if your band is just starting out and you barely have time to check out and try all the social media platforms, you could never go wrong with Facebook or Twitter. For video streaming, YouTube remains the best option. Its reach and popularity among consumers of video content are still second to none at the moment.

What you need to bear in mind in crafting your ad is that it has to be catchy enough that the likelihood of it being ignored or "scrolled up" by viewers will be very low. People's attention spans are unbelievably short these days. If you make an ad that takes more than ten seconds to actually reveal its message, you have to accept that viewers will just flick their thumbs so they can see other, more interesting visuals.

This means you have to create ads that are attractive enough that they will be hard to resist for most viewers. You cannot do this by simply posting a sentence or two about a fantastic song you recently released. There are techniques you have to learn on how to do this effectively.

Crafting Your Social Media Ads

Though this book is mainly about how to create impressive

audio, you have to compromise learning something else—creating high-resolution images or videos. Why you have to spend time learning about this is because simply telling people about your music on social media platforms, tweeting and hashtagging, or posting some poetry about it will not take you very far. You need people to pause a bit while they are scrolling up and down through their own news feeds. You must make them pay attention so they can tell their friends that your music exists.

To pull this off successfully, you need to come up with captivating visuals that can only be achieved by posting a digital poster or, better yet, a high-definition video that perfectly depicts the awesomeness of your newly released piece.

If you have no skill whatsoever in designing digital posters, you should consider hiring a graphic artist. If you have friends who are knowledgeable about this craft, now would be the time to reach out to them. If you have a bigger budget, a short video clip is something worth investing in. People prefer videos to pictures these days, so it will make your ad a few notches more attractive than the digital poster you have in mind.

If you hate the idea of spending money on these visuals, then you should consider learning how to make them yourself. If your brain handled the intensive regimen of music production, then learning the basics of video and graphics editing should be lessons that you will grasp just as easily.

The surprising thing about high resolution videos and graphics today is that you can create them even without installing additional software on your computer. For making your poster, you can use Canva, AdCreative, or Visme. All of these can be accessed online via your web browser.

With some basic dragging and dropping, you can create a presentable digital poster in a matter of minutes. For creating a video ad, you can use Adobe Spark, WeVideo, and Flyr. You should easily grasp the idea of how to use them if you are patient and persistent enough (Csutoras, 2021).

In creating either your poster or video ad, you must keep in mind that simplicity is the key. You have to give more by saying less. The simpler your ad, the better. Apart from putting the artist's name—which could be you or someone else—the hit single and album name and the portals in which you can be seen or heard should also be included in the most straightforward manner.

The few words that will be present should not get in the way of the graphics, and vice versa. The trick to achieving this smoothly is choosing the right color schemes and placing the right elements at the right angles and proportions.

This is something that could easily be a separate book in itself, but as you are someone who wants to do things on your own, you should at least learn the basics of it so you can promote your music in social media channels effectively.

Scouring Through Online Communities

Music remains the best hobby shared by people of all ages and races. Since this is a fact that nobody can dispute, you can have the fullest guarantee that social media groups created to propagate music can be easily found on the internet. You can socialize through these portals because there are hidden benefits you can utilize while navigating through them. So, should you start finding them and joining so you can promote your music aggressively?

While being aggressive is a common trait for the fiercest

warriors throughout history, as a passionate music creator, you must not resort to aggression, especially in the realms of social media and online communities. Before you start copy-pasting information about where people can listen to your music or avail themselves of your services, there are some precautionary measures you must instill in yourself.

This includes the importance of providing value to your fellow internet visitors. When you join Facebook or other social media music-oriented groups, try to be friendly and provide information that can help others solve some of their problems, then conduct subtle marketing of your music or the services you can offer.

With that strategy, you'll avoid becoming someone who takes advantage of people. You don't want anyone approaching you and selling goods that you do not find very useful. Likewise, you have to avoid doing the same.

This is something you must learn beforehand because on social media sites like Facebook, you could get banned from a community or from the entire platform if you are detected as a spammer. Posting the same comments repeatedly, especially if those people you chose are not your friends, will have you expelled in a matter of minutes (Skaf, 2014). As someone who takes your music career very seriously, this is something you must religiously remember.

Make Your Own Community First

Before you go out disturbing others on social media, the best course of action would be to make your own page or group and invite some of your friends to join. You may then ask them to invite their friends while you find new members with similar interests. Only then could you start luring other people from similar pages and start convincing them to help you propagate your music production career.

As your page grows, your marketability as a music producer will grow as well, which will pave the way for you to find clients who would pay you for your services. Similarly, you could also find people you could hire in times when you need to outsource some projects.

In growing your page, it is not simply about posting random photos or captions that you find amusing or something that tells people how great your life is. Instead of appearing to brag about what you have, a much wiser move would be to post information that could help them grow in their personal careers, or help them with any difficulties they may have.

As you master that act, you may find out eventually that expanding your reach is not just about going to people but making people come to you. You might still need to visit other pages and reach out to their members and administrators, but you will not need to do that very often since you have already grown your page to the point that the people from the other pages may have already heard about you.

You have to remember that obtaining valuable information is what drives people to seek you out. The more value they derive from you, the more they will cling to you and speak of your greatness. Without a doubt, such a tactic is a marketing strategy in itself—you are selling your skills and services without appearing to be selling anything at all.

Expand Only Through Other Similar Communities

In promoting your music as well as the related services you can offer, a targeted approach is what you should be doing. You have to know that the most profitable businesses out there only sell their goods to those who want them. So in promoting your music, you have to find social media pages that focus on exactly the kind of music you produce.

If you promote a hip-hop song on a heavy metal page, you will most likely be trash-talked by the members, and it will happen in the most brutal way. Likewise, promoting your heavy-metal songs in virtual places where the fans of Sinatra and Pavarotti are hanging out would be very unwise. So before you go about posting promotions of your musical outputs, be sure to do your homework first and find out which pages suit your preferences best.

Of course, there are plenty of social media groups out there that accept posts for all music genres. While plenty of these could be very strict in their policies, some of them would welcome you with open arms. You just have to be sure that you meet their community guidelines if you post photos, links, and any other information that is designed to lead people to your own page.

Some page administrators would see you as a competitor, and when they do, they might refrain from accepting you, or they might ban you from ever visiting their page again. This is one of the harsh realities you have to contend with while promoting your material on social media.

On Facebook, one of the advantages you might find useful is that the more you browse through pages that are similar to yours, the more you will be provided with pages that are musically themed as well. By then, connecting to other music communities should be much easier.

If you feel that your skills have attained business-level status, extending your social media reach beyond the halls of Facebook would be a great move as well. The social media platform for you to explore should be LinkedIn. This platform is very business-centric. In fact, it was crafted with business and employment as its main driving forces.

By creating a LinkedIn profile, you are also creating an online portfolio where you can post content such as articles, video tutorials, or webinars. These are also profitable avenues to explore as you expand on your income-generating feats as a music producer.

LinkedIn also has its own communities created by people of various hobbies and interests, and there are lots of musically inclined community administrators there. Joining them is not that hard, though you might have to connect with the people running them with a very business-minded approach.

Becoming a proficient music producer in these modern times involves thinking and acting like a businessman. Speaking of business, this is something we are about to discuss in this next section.

Understanding the Business Side of Music Production

To make music and get paid generously for it—there's no happier life for a musician and no better livelihood for a performer. As pure artists at heart, we dream of nothing but expressing our works of art in front of audiences, getting applauded, and getting rewarded for the hard work we do. What a magnificent way of life would it be if we, as music creators, did nothing but this on a daily basis?

As exciting as that would be, that is not how it usually works. Music production, as well as the entire realm of the music industry, is a gigantic business. No matter how loudly we might shout that "It's all about the music!" or "Artistic expression is the bottom line of it all!" such a simplistic approach is not always applicable in the real world.

Hate that truth or express your severe disgust over it, but it's just an irrefutable fact. It is understandable that you hate admitting that the music world revolves around money. Sadly, you just have to accept that it is the truth.

Money and Passion: The Delicate Balance

Most likely, you have an intense urge to whine and complain about that title. Instead of whining about it, would it not be wiser if you resort instead to some strategies that will work to your advantage? Since the music industry is largely about financial gain, at least for most people, why can't we just come up with a set of tactics that will funnel some of that money in our direction?

But maybe you are not interested in making lots of money since all you care about is making your music heard. Fine. But you have to accept that in order to make people listen, you have to bring music to the right ears, and that requires money.

So, as painful and disappointing as that may be to you, you might as well accept it. Since the music industry highly requires finances so it can remain functional, you have to raise enough of it so you can get your music across to your audience.

The reason why some pop stars became insanely rich and famous is because their music was placed on platforms where plenty of people could hear and see them. Without the promotional powers of such platforms, there would be no Beatles, Elvis Presley, Michael Jackson, or any other famous music icon you can think of.

Based on that notion, as a passionate music creator, you must concede to the reality that you need to make money and raise funds—so you can pay for the social media promotion strategies mentioned earlier, and the processing fees needed to publish your music on audio-streaming platforms. Also, do not forget about all the other gear and equipment you need to buy so you can become a prolific music producer.

It is a serious livelihood that you are trying to head for, something that you hope will become your main day job that can provide you sustenance. Naturally, such an endeavor does not come for free, nor does it come cheap. There are ways to make it less costly, but you just have to acknowledge beforehand that this career you are trying to build comes with a price.

Marketing for the Sake of Familiarity

So, music production is a business, and you need money to propagate your music. What should you do about it then? There is a direct approach, while there is also a subtle approach. You can do both, or you can do just one, preferably the first one mentioned. The direct approach is to perform live or through video streaming.

Being direct also means delivering your music to people in a straightforward manner. This means selling your musicianship or the recorded version of your music. But being effective with that means you have to think and act like a salesman—you have to convince people that your music is worth paying for.

So how do you do that? Simple—you have to make your music as attractive as possible to listeners. When that happens, people will listen to you, share your music, and bring in more listeners, which could usher in a lot of money. You do not want it, but we already acknowledge that you do need it to promote your music to a wider audience.

But how do you make your music more attractive? We already learned how to produce music that people would want to listen to in the previous chapters. If you paid enough attention, you should be very capable of creating quality recorded music by now. But there is another element you need to have, and it can only be attained through the power of familiarity.

In the field of entertainment, familiarity is a huge thing, especially in the music industry. There must have been times you wondered why a brilliantly crafted song did not become popular while a crappy tune with terrible lyrics became a global sensation.

This is because of the mesmerizing effect of familiarity. Because that ugly tune was played again and again and was listened to by people in various avenues, the song became irresistibly familiar. There might only be a very low level of artistry in that song. But because of the constant playback, it got to the ears of the masses, and the song became mysteriously attractive to everyone's taste (Ward et al., 2013).

No matter how you may rant about how your song is not more popular than that ugly hymn, people love that song because, as the saying goes, "It is familiar to millions." This should make it much clearer that, in executing the promotional methods you have learned so far, we need money to promote your music. The reason? Familiarity.

You cannot establish yourself as a hitmaker if people are not familiar with your tunes. And if you want to make that happen, you need to earn money so you can promote your craft and make your songs irresistibly familiar. There is no better way to convince people that you can give them their money's worth, in addition to the good music that you produce, of course.

Whether you prefer performing live or just selling your music through online platforms, one thing is for sure—you have to prove that you are attractive to the audience. No matter how passionate you are about what you do, you will not be doing that for a very long time without the financial sustenance you need to keep going. Behind the success of every famous musician is a business mechanism that works in the background. Accept it or ignore it. But if you are sincere about your career goals, you have to adhere to the first option.

Content Creation: Something to Consider As a Music Producer

Let us get to it directly—this is about blogging, vlogging, or any kind of online content creation. Why should you be considering this? Because plenty of musicians are doing it and have been raking in great financial rewards in addition to the music we hear and the live performances they do.

Why vlogging or blogging are also worthwhile investments of your time and resources is because, in addition to using these platforms to promote your stuff, you could also earn from them through advertising and affiliate marketing.

You have probably seen plenty of musicians who present

themselves on YouTube as content creators as well. While you might simply see them as people with the willingness to teach, what they are actually doing is selling their products and services, or those of other businesses as well.

While they are explaining the music-related lessons they give, you will surely hear them talking about certain products such as musical instruments, sound equipment, and all sorts of digital tools that people could buy from the affiliate links they give in the description boxes of their videos.

As a passionate music artist, you might hate the idea of selling to people. But again, thinking like a businessman is something you must embrace because, after all, making a living out of music is something you have been dreaming of for a long time already.

If you have some writing skills or if you love the idea of people reading about your knowledge and experiences, you should start a blog that speaks about your music-production journey. If you hate writing but would like to appear on a video as you teach your musical skills and secrets to others, then vlogging is the better path to take.

Though most of the professional vloggers you see have expensive video equipment in their arsenal, you do not really need this to start vlogging. You can start just by using your phone, even if all you have are some basic videography skills under your belt.

Basic videoing skills and sound recording, which you are already very good at, are all that you really need to become an excellent vlogger. Most of the richest YouTubers today started this way, and if you do the same, vlogging success should not be that far ahead.

Podcasting is also something worth considering. If you hate writing and if you do not have the guts to be captured through video while explaining something, how about recording your voice so people can hear it the way they listen to your songs?

Podcasting is among the most popular pastimes for those who want to learn something while driving, working out, or doing household chores. It is a very lucrative avenue for online content creators, and in promoting your musical skills and services, the digital-age version of radio broadcasting must be something you should explore as well (Polner, 2022).

Other Ways of Generating Income

If you are not interested in any of the money-making tips mentioned above, fret not; there are still other ways to earn. If content creation is not your thing, you might want to consider selling music-related merchandise instead. There are two ideal ways of doing this: putting up your own online store or by using your own social media page to sell products to your members and visitors.

Though you might find it too technical, building an online store is not really as hard as you think. With platforms such as Shopify, WooCommerce, and Wix, you can be fully set for selling in a few hours, provided you have already accomplished certain requirements (Glover, 2019).

If you find that too burdensome, then selling via your existing Facebook page might be a bit more convenient. With Facebook's marketplace features, you can start selling right away. This of course requires plenty of effort, since selling is an art you must master to become truly effective at it.

So what products should you be selling? Since you work with

musical artists, selling their merchandise would be ideal. T-shirts, towels, bracelets, and CDs and DVDs containing their music would be the best bets.

If you hate the mere act of selling, then you should ditch these ideas altogether. Still, these ideas must be included because they are meant to be here. Though they are not really related to music production in a direct sense, they are crucial for someone who wishes to be profitable in the music industry. You must acknowledge that this path you are taking has a business side. You must participate in it so you can make it through the years.

Collaborating With Other Musicians and Producers

If you ask for some success tips from very successful people in any particular field you may think of, most of them will surely offer you advice on how to build your network. This is what the next lesson is all about. In order to become a profitable music entity, you have to learn how to become a people person.

We have already acknowledged that this industry you hopped into is a business. In this section, let us educate ourselves on how to work in tandem with other artists and music producers. No business will ever thrive if buying, selling, and collaborating do not happen, and for that reason, this next discussion should matter to you.

No matter how religiously you absorb the lessons you learned so far, they all amount to nothing if you cannot master the art of collaboration. So do your damnedest to take notes on what you are about to learn. It does not need to be taken literally, though; a mental note of the following will be totally fine.

Prioritize Artistry Over Money

The most proficient people in the field of music consider themselves artists, nothing more, nothing less. While plenty of them might also be exceptional at doing other things, they prioritize their artistry over anything else. Hopefully, they are paid massive amounts due to their skills, but it took them a while to achieve that level of profitability. Before they became national or global sensations, they were nobodies, just like you and me.

As the days and years rolled on while they mastered their craft, they attained the level of notoriety that they now enjoy. They are viewed as figures of high market value because of the fame they achieved, and the reason for that is due to intense hard work, dedication, and truckloads of discipline.

Yes, not all pop stars are exceptionally talented. A lot of them are overrated. There are also those who only became famous because of their good looks. But musical artists in this category had only luck under their belt. Are you willing to stake your success while waiting for your chance to get lucky? While it is indeed true that some artists only became iconic because of a stroke of luck, we cannot deny that there are plenty of others who became successful because of unparalleled hard work.

Artistry, at its most impeccable level, can never be attained without intensive effort. So if you are adamant about your goal of becoming a marketable music producer, focus on being an exceptional artist first. People within the music network will begin to notice you in no time. By then, you will not need to approach them for work; they will come to you and ask you to work with them!

Connect With People Who Share The Same Vision

If we ask any successful person how a network must be built, they will surely elaborate further by saying you should get along with like-minded people who share the same vision. Like asking a person who is emotionally and mentally compatible with your personality for marriage, you should only approach musicians with the same goals as yours and work with them.

Of course, it is not exactly like marriage, in which you will be tied to that person for life, so it should not really be that big of a deal. But there will be times when working on a project will consume weeks or months of your precious time. So by all means, do your homework and do some evaluation on what working with some particular musicians would be like and how easy or hard they are to get along with.

Apart from the difficulty or ease they might give you, you must also ask a more vital question, do they share the same vision? Are they willing to go in the direction that you as an artist are heading for? Since you are passionate about what you do, the best path would be toward those who are equally passionate people as well. And if they are as passionate as you, they will most certainly have goals that they are not willing to compromise on.

To put it into perspective, remind yourself that your music is a work of art. Because you want your musical outputs to speak for your reputation. Would you be willing to work on projects that will only tarnish your credibility? If you are someone who only works for the sake of money, you will be inclined to say yes. But since you acknowledged that artistry must be prioritized in building your connections, be principled enough to back down from working with people who will only smear the good name you tried so hard to establish.

So in deciding to collaborate with others, do your best to identify those who share the same vision. Nothing feels better than getting the financial rewards you aim for while doing it under a very smooth working relationship. Such a setting will be very fun and emotionally uplifting. You can never say no to that, can you?

Grab Your Share, Pull Your Own Weight

Being in a big business such as the one we are a part of includes grabbing shares. Money, fame, power—these are, without a doubt, parts of this massive industry we are currently working with. There is absolutely nothing wrong if you grab your fair share of those three aspects. As long as you do not abuse or overuse them or trample on anyone as you grab your slice of the pie, you are simply executing justice on your own terms.

We are talking about grabbing your share as a music collaborator here, and in that context, you have to also grab your share of the workload. In every workforce, whether within the field of music or outside of it, there are plenty of people who want to reap huge monetary rewards but will avoid the heavy lifting when the need for it shows up.

Project success will not happen if workers think and behave that way. Would you be willing to work with people like that? If you understood the previous tip well enough, you should avoid working with people who are not willing to go where you are heading, and in that regard, you must avoid those who are not willing to perform their rightful duties. Similarly, you must do your part as well, with the highest level of wholeheartedness.

Success in any business deal only happens satisfactorily if tasks are well-assigned and if all the stakeholders will pour out the strength and resources required of them. You should pour out yours in the most satisfactory manner at all times. Failing to do so would weaken the network you are trying to build, and that would be utterly bad for business.

Execute the Real Essence of Loyalty

Plenty of businesses are built on relationships. It might not be the cuddling-romancing kind, but good relationships are among the crucial nuts and bolts that keep multi-billion dollar businesses on track. Without them, the wheels and cogs that keep them running would stop functioning, and the evident profitability would not have happened.

One of the most vital elements of a good relationship is loyalty. If you want to view yourself as a good businessman, you have to remain loyal to those who deserve it, so you can be treated with the same level of loyalty you show to others. It is highly true that some businessmen will easily dump you if you are no longer capable of serving their interests. But if you are truly honest with yourself, would you not do the same?

Since we understand already that connecting with people who share the same vision is vital for our success, we have to acknowledge that being with someone who offers no contribution to what we do is a waste of time. Therefore, we cannot blame those who avoid us if we are not helpful to them in any way.

What we are trying to imply here is that loyalty must be given in accordance with what you need, what they need, and what a certain objective requires. In the field of business, loyalty must come with a price; it should be served under certain circumstances. As long as you understand the lessons mentioned above, it is highly unlikely that you will fail to execute loyalty in the fairest manner imaginable.

CONCLUSION

The latest breakthroughs of the digital age have paved the way for a lot of methods that have made our lives very convenient. Such a level of convenience has made its way into the once complex and difficult field of music production. Because of the presence of computerized methods, the way musicians and record producers make and distribute music has been fully revolutionized.

Gone are the days when music enthusiasts would have to purchase massive, expensive equipment or wait for the approval of wealthy business executives in the music business. All that is needed is a little budget and the guts to participate in the ever-expanding realm of modern music, which becomes more dynamic and more engaging with each passing day.

Plenty of successful pop stars today are DIY musicians who make music at home inside their own music studios, right inside their bedrooms. With a computer and some inexpensive audio equipment, they can record their tracks, mix their music, and release their soon-to-be hits independently.

Even without the help of major record labels, their hit songs are propagated on the airwaves as well as in the virtual domain of cyberspace. Because such an occurrence has become very common, many young musicians have grabbed their rightful share of this magnificent phenomenon.

Since all of those digital-age musicians are producing music from their homes, you too have grabbed every possible learning material that can help you reach the success you greatly aspired for. Consequently, you had a chance to grab this book and have learned its simple and comprehensive lessons.

As a home-based, independent music producer, there are

skills you need to acquire and bits of knowledge that you have to enhance. Among these is learning how to operate a DAW so that the music you create can be rendered electronically and you can shape it to perfection with your digital tools.

You also have to train your ears to figure out how a certain sound or frequency can be modified so it sounds impressive when mixed together with other audio elements. In the process of doing so, you've come to understand that balance and harmony must be exercised at all times so that a song can be heard in its most beautiful form.

After learning the skills needed to create impressive music, you learned that it was not the end of it all. You embraced the fact that there is a business side to music production and that you have to adapt to the realities that govern it.

Money is not really something most musicians are overly concerned with. But as one who wants to make a living out of music, you have acknowledged that you need to compromise and find ways to earn so that your music production skills, which you now see as a means of living, can thrive through the years.

In order for your business to grow, you need to collaborate with other people of similar interests. Dealing with them involves doing things that you do not totally like. You accept, however, that such things are necessary because of your burning passion for making it in the music industry.

Promotional tactics are also among the things to learn and implement in your music career. Because the internet is a dimension that keeps on expanding day by day, there are countless avenues on it that you need to explore so you can use them to bring your musical creations to various audiences.

As you grow in your newfound career, you have to bear in mind that the field of music production, as well as the entire realm of the music industry, will undergo significant changes as the next decades roll on. The methods and skills you learned here might be the current industry standards, but in the next few years, they might be outdated already.

As a precaution, you have to do your best to be competitive at all times. The very best in the industry have an unquenchable thirst for learning something new. You, as a "recently knighted" music producer, should not think too differently. You have to attain that trait as well.

There will always be exciting tools to learn about, and there will always be new kinds of digital mechanisms that will be applicable to your musical endeavors. Be willing to explore new methods, never stop collaborating with other music lovers, work with passion, and most importantly, NEVER STOP LEARNING.

So, this was music production for beginners. Are you ready to take it to the next level? If you've got what it takes, then check out my next book in the series "music production for professionals 2024".

Swindali
www.swindali.com

GLOSSARY

Amplitude: A sound property that determines how we perceive the loudness of sound due to the relative transmission of sound waves.

Analog: A stream of continuous audio waves that can be interpreted into electronic signals and transformed into a certain kind of information. It is also referred to as the opposite of digital.

Audio Clipping: A waveform distortion that results from excessive signal amplification of an audio track.

Audio Interface: A device designed to convert sound signals from musical instruments and microphones into a digital format that can be rendered by a computer.

CPU (Central Processing Unit): The main processor chip of a computer. It can also be defined as the brain of the computer.

DAW (Digital Audio Workspace): A computer software application that acts as a digital version of a recording studio.

Decibel (dB): A unit for measuring the relative loudness of sound.

DIY (Do It Yourself): A term used for the general method of fixing, hobbies, and tutorials that could be done by anyone single handedly.

Equalizer (EQ): An audio filtering device that can boost frequencies by isolating them. Virtual EQs are now included in all digital music software as a built-in component.

FLAC (Free Lossless Audio Codec): An open-source audio file type that renders no loss of quality even after compression. It is similar to MP3.

GB (Gigabyte): The standard unit used in digitization to measure file storage capacity.

GHz (Gigahertz): The standard unit used in digitization to measure data transfer and overall processing speed.

Metronome: A rehearsal tool used by musicians to play accurately by means of steady beats or rhythmic pulses.

MIDI (Musical Instrument Digital Interface): A computer interface that allows analog music to be processed digitally. It is now an umbrella term for any kind of music that can be crafted within a computer system.

MP4A (Mpeg Layer 4 Audio): A sound format very similar to MP3, but with a higher level of bit rate and overall quality.

Percussions: Instruments that can be played by hitting and striking, such as drums, gongs, cymbals, etc.

Plug-in: A software extension that adds more functionalities to an existing host program.

Pre-amp: An audio amplifier that enhances a weak electronic signal without compromising sound quality.

RAM (Random Access Memory): A circuit board with memory chips that store data temporarily. It is one of the most vital components that determines how fast a computer can process data.

Software Interface: A component of software applications that allows human users to interact with a computer system.

Sound Diffuser: An insulator used in recording studios that can reduce the intensity of reflected sound.

Synthesizer: A digital musical instrument, such as a keyboard, that can simulate various electronic sounds during a recording session.

Virtual Instrument: A virtual representation of a musical instrument in a computer system.

VST (Virtual Studio Technology): The umbrella term for software technology that encompasses DAWs and VSTIs in general.

Vocal Booth: A small cubicle where singers can be isolated and sing freely away from background noise.

Waveform: A graphical representation of a sound wave. It is also the representation of how strong or weak a recorded audio clip is when displayed on a digital display.

MUSIC PRODUCTION | 2024+ EDITION

INTRODUCTION

Music production is a fascinating and constantly evolving field that combines technical knowledge and creativity to create amazing works of art. Whether you're an aspiring producer or an experienced musician looking to take your skills to the next level, there's always something new to learn and explore.

However, music production can also be challenging, especially for those who are just starting out. The technical aspects of the craft can be overwhelming, and the cost of high-end equipment and professional studio space can be a significant barrier to entry. Additionally, the highly competitive nature of the music industry can make it difficult to find opportunities to gain hands-on experience and succeed in the field.

But don't worry—there is a solution. In this book, we offer a comprehensive guide to music production that covers everything from the basics of recording and mixing to the latest trends in the industry. Authored by a team of experienced music producers and engineers, this book is designed to be an essential resource for anyone who wants to succeed in the world of music production.

One of the biggest challenges facing learners in the field of music production is the technical knowledge required to succeed. In this book, we break down the technical aspects of music production into easy-to-understand terms, so you can learn at your own pace and build a solid foundation of knowledge. We cover everything from signal flow and microphone placement to equalization and compression, so you can start producing high-quality music right away.

Another challenge facing aspiring music producers is the cost of high-end equipment and professional studio space. In this book, we offer guidance on how to access and use professional equipment, including tips on how to find affordable gear and how to make the most of what you have. We also cover how to build a home studio or find professional studio space, so you can start producing music in a professional environment without breaking the bank.

Networking is also an essential aspect of succeeding in the music industry. In this book, we offer tips on how to network with other professionals in the industry and find opportunities to gain hands-on experience, such as internships or apprenticeships. We will also cover how to succeed in a highly competitive industry, including strategies for marketing and promoting your music, and building a successful career as a music producer.

Finally, we will cover the latest trends and technology in the music industry, so you can stay up-to-date on the latest techniques and equipment. We also offer guidance on how to keep up with industry trends and technology, so you can continue to grow and evolve as a music producer.

Ultimately, this book is designed to be a comprehensive

guide to music production. It will help you overcome common complaints and problems when learning about an advanced, professional career in music production. We promise to increase your chances of success in the industry by providing you with a wealth of knowledge that can be used as a curriculum. Whether you're a beginner or an experienced music producer, this book is a must-have resource for anyone who is serious about succeeding in the world of music production.

So what are you waiting for? Let's get started so that you can learn to produce amazing music today!

A Brief History of Music Production

Music production is the process of creating and recording music. Before the invention of recording technology, music was primarily performed live in various settings. The phonograph was invented in the late 19th century, allowing for the recording and playback of music for the first time. The development of electrical recording technology in the 1920s improved the quality of recorded music. The 1940s saw the development of magnetic tape, which revolutionized music production by allowing multi-track recording and editing. The 1980s saw the widespread adoption of digital recording technology, which provided even greater control over the production process and higher-quality sound. The rise of home recording studios and the internet have changed the way music is consumed and distributed. The widespread availability of affordable digital audio workstations has made music production more accessible than ever before. To this day, music production continues to evolve through new technologies and techniques.

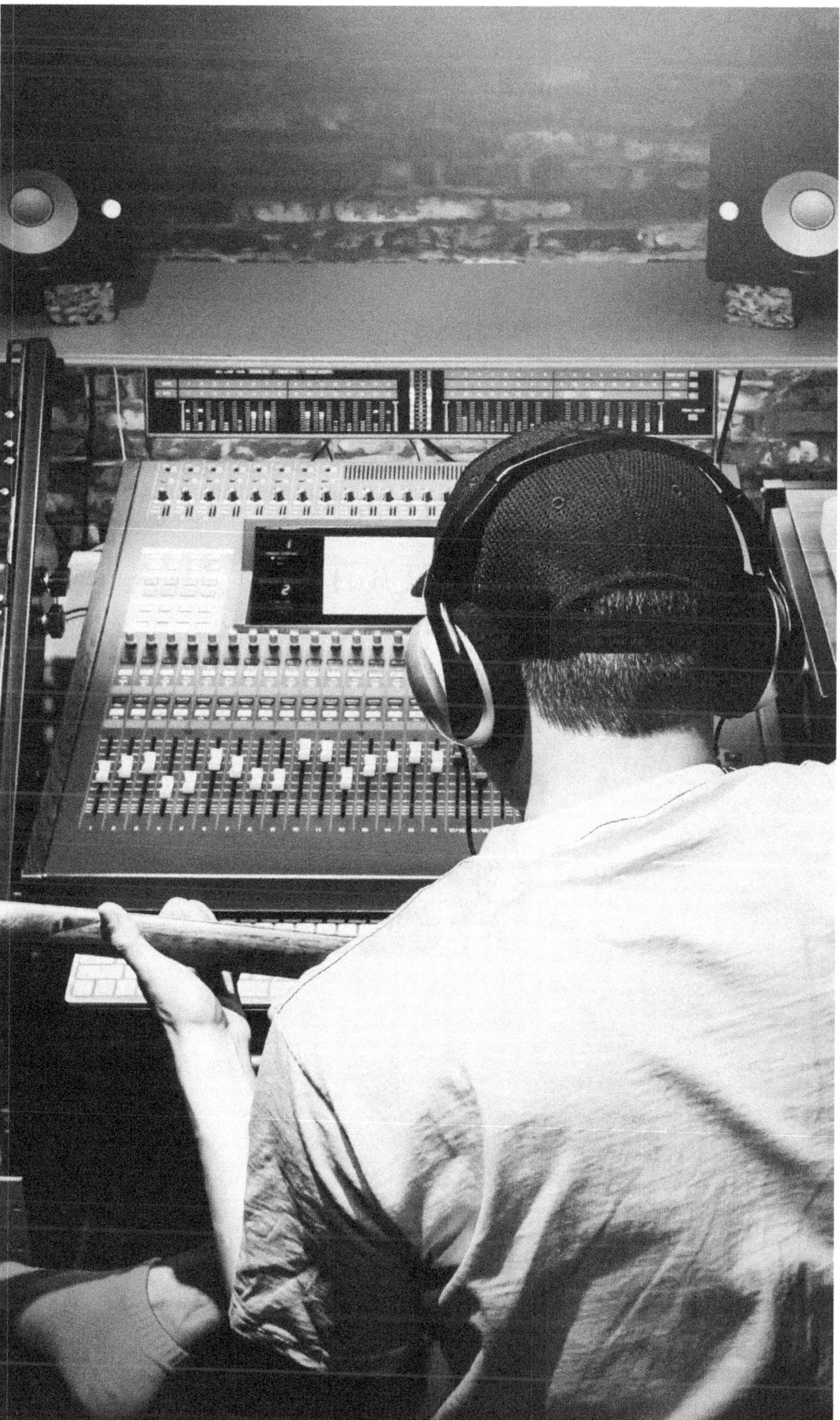

CHAPTER 1

MUSIC PRODUCTION AS A CAREER

Music production is the process of creating and recording music. This can involve composing or arranging music, recording and editing audio, mixing and mastering, and preparing the final product for distribution. Music production can take place in a variety of settings, from professional recording studios to home-based setups. Studio recording refers to the process of recording audio in a controlled environment, typically a recording studio. This can involve the use of professional audio equipment, including microphones, mixers, and digital audio workstations (DAWs), to capture and edit audio recordings. Studio recording allows for precise control over the sound and quality of recorded audio, making it a popular choice for professional music production. To better understand studio recording and all these other concepts, let's take a closer look at having a career in music production, as well as its importance to the industry.

Overview of Music Production as a Career

Music production is a complex and ever-evolving field that requires a high level of technical expertise, creativity, and dedication to master. For those who are passionate about music and possess (or are willing to cultivate) a strong skill set in audio engineering and production, a career in professional music production can offer a wide range of opportunities.

Advanced music production careers typically require a strong foundation in music theory and composition, as well as a deep understanding of the technical aspects of recording, mixing, and mastering. Professionals in this field often have years of experience working with a variety of audio equipment, DAWs, and software, as well as a deep understanding of various music genres and production techniques.

One of the most important aspects of a career in professional music production is the ability to stay up-to-date with the latest trends and technologies in the industry. This often requires ongoing training and education, as well as a willingness to try new things. Many professionals in this field attend industry conferences and workshops, participate in online forums and discussion groups, and network with other professionals to stay on top of the latest developments in the field.

There are many different career paths available in professional music production, including roles as:

- Recording engineers,
- Mix engineers,
- Mastering engineers,
- Music producers,
- Sound designers
- Music for motion picture

Recording engineers are responsible for capturing high-quality audio recordings in a studio or live setting, while mix engineers are responsible for blending and balancing individual tracks to create a cohesive, polished sound. Mastering engineers are responsible for putting the finishing touches on a recording, ensuring that it sounds great on a variety of playback systems.

Music producers are responsible for overseeing the entire production process, from songwriting and composition to recording and mixing. They work closely with artists and other professionals to create a unique and compelling sound that reflects the artist's vision and style. Sound designers, on the other hand, create and manipulate sound effects and other audio elements for use in film, television, video games, and other media.

The demand for skilled professionals in the field of music production continues to grow, with many opportunities available in a variety of settings. These may include commercial recording studios, post-production houses, broadcasting and media companies, and freelance opportunities in a variety of fields.

A career in professional music production can be highly rewarding for those with a passion for music and a strong set of technical skills. With a commitment to ongoing education and a willingness to adapt to new technologies and techniques, those pursuing this field can look forward to a long and successful career in an exciting and ever-changing industry.

The Importance of Music Production in the Industry

Music production is a vital component of the music industry, as it plays a crucial role in creating, recording, and distributing music to listeners around the world. Without music production, it would be impossible for artists to bring their musical ideas to life and share their music with a wider audience.

One of the most significant contributions of music production is its ability to shape and define the sound of a recording. Skilled producers can work with artists to help them refine their musical ideas, select the right instrumentation and equipment, and create a cohesive, polished sound that resonates with listeners. Through careful production techniques such as mixing and mastering, producers can enhance the clarity and balance of a recording, allowing each individual element to shine through and create a powerful and immersive listening experience.

In addition to its artistic contributions, music production also plays a crucial role in the business side of the music industry. Producers work closely with record labels, distributors, and other industry professionals to ensure that music is produced and distributed in a way that maximizes its commercial potential. This can involve everything from selecting the right release date and marketing strategy to negotiating licensing deals and managing the logistics of physical distribution.

The importance of music production in the modern era cannot be overstated. With the advent of digital technology and the internet, more and more artists are able to produce and distribute their own music independently. This has created an explosion of new music and talent, and has given rise to a new generation of producers who are able to work in a variety of genres and styles.

At the same time, however, the democratization of music production has also made it more important than ever for artists and producers to have a deep understanding of the technical and business aspects of the music industry. With so many different tools and platforms available, it can be difficult to navigate the complexities of music production and distribution without the right knowledge and support.

From its artistic contributions to its business and commercial applications, music production is a vital component of the industry that helps to shape the sound and culture of music around the world. As the industry continues to evolve, the role of music production will become even more important, and the demand for skilled producers who can navigate the complex landscape of the music industry will continue to grow.

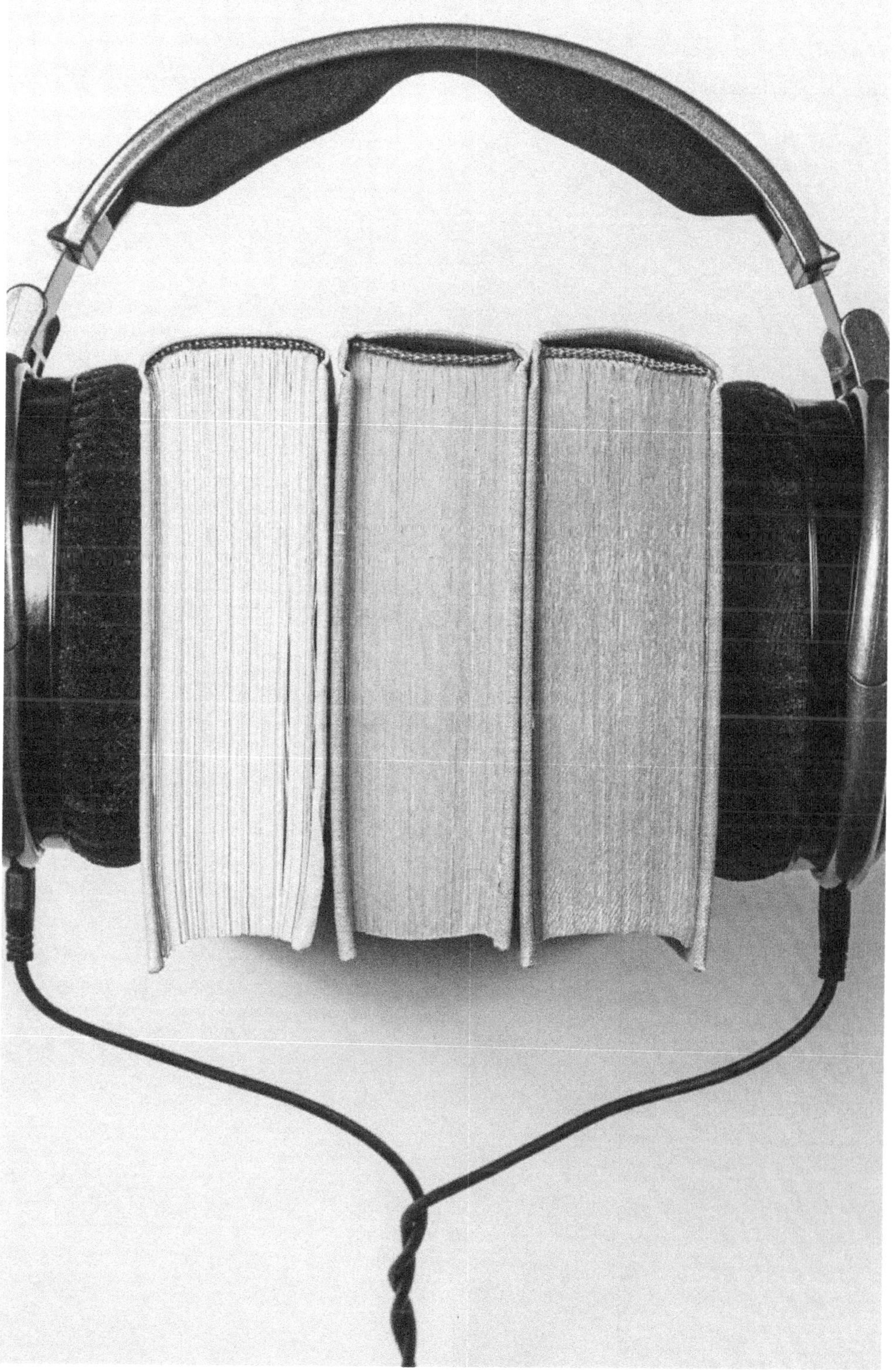

CHAPTER 2
GETTING EDUCATED

While this book is a comprehensive guide to music production, it's important to note that formal education can also be valuable. As is the case when you are learning to play the guitar, reading a book can provide you with a foundation of knowledge, but it's practice and instruction from a professional that will truly allow you to master the craft. Similarly, music production requires practice and familiarity with equipment, and this book can certainly help with that. However, formal education can accelerate the learning process even further.

Plus, if you're interested in pursuing a career in music production, a formal degree or diploma is more or less essential. Formal education provides a deeper understanding of music theory, technical skills, and the industry as a whole. This comprehensive understanding can be invaluable for career advancement.

So, while this book is an excellent resource, it's important to consider supplementing it with formal education. By doing so, you can gain a well-rounded education and become a more competitive candidate in the music industry.

Now, let's take a closer look at getting educated!

Educational Options and Requirements

Whether you're interested in recording and producing music in a professional studio or working as an independent producer, there are a variety of educational options available to help you develop the skills and knowledge.

One of the most popular paths to a career in music production is through a degree program. Many universities and colleges offer programs in music production or audio engineering, which can provide students with a comprehensive education in the technical aspects of music production. These programs typically cover topics such as recording techniques, mixing and mastering, music theory, and studio equipment. They often include hands-on experience working with industry-standard software and hardware.

The specific requirements for studying music production at a university may vary depending on the institution and the program. However, here are some common requirements that you may encounter:

- **Educational background:** Many music production programs require applicants to have a high school diploma or equivalent.
- **Musical ability:** While it's not always a requirement, having some level of musical ability can be beneficial for studying music production. This can include playing an instrument, singing, or having a general understanding of music theory.
- **Portfolio or audition:** Some music production programs may require applicants to submit a portfolio of their work or participate in an audition to demonstrate their technical and creative abilities.

- **Letters of recommendation:** Some universities may require letters of recommendation from teachers, mentors, or other professionals in the music industry.
- **Application materials:** Applicants will typically need to submit an application form, transcripts, and a personal statement outlining their goals and reasons for wanting to study music production.

Another option for those interested in music production is attending a vocational or technical school. These programs are often shorter in duration than traditional degree programs and focus more specifically on the practical aspects of music production, such as recording techniques and equipment operation. Vocational and technical schools can be a great choice for those who want to enter the workforce quickly and have a more hands-on approach to learning.

There are also many online courses and tutorials available for those who want to learn music production on their own. These courses often provide in-depth instruction on specific topics like mixing and mastering, and can be a great way to develop your skills at your own pace.

Regardless of the educational path you choose, it's important to remember that music production is a constantly evolving field, and that ongoing learning and professional development is key to success. Attending industry conferences, workshops, and seminars, as well as staying up-to-date with the latest software and hardware, can help you stay at the forefront of the field and remain competitive in the job market.

Whether you choose to pursue a degree program, attend a vocational school, or learn on your own through online courses, the key is to focus on developing the technical skills and creative talents that will allow you to succeed in this dynamic and rewarding field.

The Role of Apprenticeships and Internships

An apprenticeship is a structured training program that combines on-the-job learning with classroom instruction. In the music industry, apprenticeships are provided by recording studios, production companies, and other music-related businesses. Apprenticeships typically last for a set period of time, and may involve working under the guidance of an experienced music producer or engineer.

Internships, on the other hand, are typically short-term and may or may not be paid. Internships provide an opportunity for students or recent graduates to gain practical experience in a professional setting. Internships can also be provided by recording studios, music production companies, and other music industry businesses. Interns may assist with various tasks such as recording sessions, equipment setup, and administrative duties.

Both apprenticeships and internships offer valuable opportunities to learn from experienced music industry professionals, and can help aspiring music producers build their skills and knowledge. Additionally, these programs can provide access to industry contacts and networking opportunities, which can be crucial for building a successful career in music production.

While apprenticeships and internships can be valuable for gaining hands-on experience, they are not a substitute for formal education or training. Apprenticeships and internships should be seen as complementary to education, and can provide an opportunity to put classroom learning into practice.

Apprenticeships and internships can play an important role in launching a career in music production. These programs provide hands-on experience and training in a professional setting, and can help aspiring music producers build their skills and knowledge. If you're interested in pursuing a career in music production, consider seeking out apprenticeships or internships in the industry to gain valuable experience and industry contacts.

The Importance of Networking and Relationships

Networking and building relationships are essential parts of establishing a successful career in music production. In the music industry, it's not only what you know, but whom you know that can make a difference in your career prospects. Many of these relationships can be established with teachers and fellow students at an educational facility.

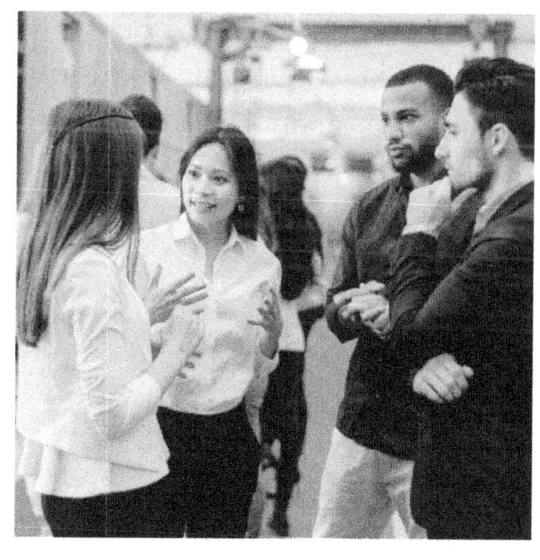

Building relationships in the music industry can help you get your foot in the door, find job opportunities, and gain access to resources and information that can be helpful in your career. This can include meeting other music producers, engineers, musicians, and industry professionals at events such as conferences, trade shows, and concerts. Networking can also involve reaching out to professionals in the industry through email, social media, or other channels.

Maintaining existing relationships is also important. This can involve keeping in touch with contacts, following up after meetings, and staying up-to-date on industry trends and developments. Building relationships with others in the music industry can help you stay connected to opportunities and stay informed about industry changes.

Networking and building relationships can also lead to collaborations and creative partnerships. For example, meeting a talented musician or artist could lead to a collaboration on a new project. Building relationships with other music producers or engineers can also provide opportunities for sharing knowledge and learning from others in the industry.

One way to network and build relationships is by joining professional organizations which can provide access to industry events, training and educational opportunities, and networking events with other professionals in the industry.

Consider attending industry events, joining professional organizations, and reaching out to other professionals in the industry to build your network and open doors to new opportunities.

CHAPTER 3
THE STUDIO ENVIRONMENT

In this chapter, we will look at studio design, acoustics, and equipment as well as learn how to set up and manage your very own professional studio.

Studio Design and Acoustics

When it comes to music production, the studio's design and acoustics are two critical factors that can significantly impact the final recording. A well-designed studio with proper acoustics can make all the difference in creating high-quality music recordings. Let's look at how professionals optimize these two elements to create the best quality recordings they can.

Studio Design

Studio design encompasses the layout, size, and shape of the recording space, along with the equipment and materials used. The design of a recording studio can influence the sound quality and overall workflow of music production. Here are some key factors to consider when designing a recording studio:

- The size and shape of the room can affect the way that sound waves behave within it. A larger room with higher ceilings will have a longer reverb time than a smaller room with lower ceilings. The shape of the room can also affect the acoustics, with rectangular rooms being the most ideal.

- Soundproofing is critical to preventing external noise from interfering with the recording process. Materials such as acoustic foam, mass-loaded vinyl, and resilient channels can be used to minimize sound transmission.
- Room treatment involves the placement of acoustic panels and diffusers to manage the sound waves within the room. This can help to reduce standing waves, echoes, and other unwanted acoustic anomalies.
- The placement of equipment within the studio can also affect the sound quality. For example, the position of the monitors and microphones can significantly impact the recording quality.

Acoustics

Acoustics is the study of sound, and how it changes in different places or environments. In a music production setting, acoustics can significantly impact the quality of the recordings. This is how professionals optimize their studio to get the best acoustic quality:

- **Speaker placement:** The placement of the studio monitors is crucial to ensure accurate sound reproduction. The monitors should be placed at ear level and positioned in a way that minimizes reflections from walls, ceilings, and floors.
- **Bass traps:** These are sound-absorbing panels which are specifically created to capture and reduce the impact of low-frequency sounds. Placing bass traps in the corners of the room can help to reduce bass buildup and improve the

overall sound quality.

- **Diffusion:** This is the scattering of sound waves to create a more even distribution of sound within the room. Diffusers can be placed on walls and ceilings to create a more natural and balanced sound.
- **Microphone placement:** Proper microphone placement is crucial to achieving the desired sound quality. Placing the microphone too close to walls or corners can result in unwanted reflections and resonances.

Keep in mind that every recording space is unique, and it may take some experimentation to find the optimal setup for your specific needs. With careful planning and attention to detail, high-quality recording space can be achieved, providing a foundation for creating great music.

Importance of Equipment and Gear Selection

The equipment and gear that you use in music production can significantly impact the quality of your recordings. The quality of the microphones, preamps, compressors, and other equipment can affect the overall tone, dynamics, and clarity of your recordings. High-quality gear can help you achieve a more polished and professional sound, while lower quality equipment can result in a weaker and less defined sound.

Types of Equipment and Gear

There are many different types of equipment and gear used in music production. The equipment you use will depend on your style of music, budget, and personal tastes. Consider viewing demos at specialized shops to figure out which equipment best suits your needs. Here are some of the most common types of equipment used in music production:

- **Computer and DAW:** The computer is the heart of the studio, and the DAW is the software used to record, edit, and mix music. A DAW is essentially a virtual studio that includes tools for recording, arranging, editing, and mixing audio.
- **Audio interface:** This is a device that connects your computer to other audio equipment, such as microphones, instruments, and speakers. It converts analog signals from your equipment into digital signals that can be processed by the computer.
- **Microphones:** These are used to capture sound from various sources, such as vocals, instruments, and drums. There are different types of microphones, including condenser, dynamic, and ribbon microphones. Each of these has unique sound characteristics.
- **Monitors:** These are speakers designed specifically for music production. They provide accurate sound reproduction and are essential for monitoring and mixing music.
- **Headphones:** This is an essential tool for music production, particularly for monitoring and mixing. They provide a more detailed and focused listening experience, and can help identify imperfections that may not be noticeable with speakers.
- **MIDI Keyboard Controller:** These are used to control virtual instruments and other software-based music tools. It allows you to play and record notes, chords, and melodies into your DAW.
- **Synthesizers and Sound Modules:** These are used to create electronic sounds and textures that can be incorporated into music productions.

- **Preamps and Channel Strips:** This is used to amplify and shape the sound of microphones and other sources before they are recorded into the DAW. They can add warmth, depth, and character to recordings.
- **Compressors:** These are used to control the dynamic range of audio recordings. They can make the quieter sounds louder, and the louder sounds quieter, resulting in a more consistent sound.
- **Equalizers:** Equalizers are used to adjust the tonal balance of recordings. They allow you to adjust the frequency response of recordings to improve their clarity and balance.

These are just a few examples of the many types of equipment and gear used in music production. Each piece of gear plays a unique role in the production process, and selecting the right gear can significantly impact the quality of your recordings.

Selecting the Right Equipment and Gear

Here are some tips to help you choose the right gear:

- **Determine your needs:** Start by determining what kind of music you want to produce and what equipment you will need to achieve that sound. Consider the instruments and sounds you will be recording and the type of music you want to create.

- **Set a budget:** Once you have determined your needs, set a budget. High-quality gear can be expensive, so it's essential to establish how much you are willing to spend.
- **Conduct research:** Research the different brands and models of equipment to determine which ones will meet your needs and fit within your budget. Look for reviews and online forums, and ask for recommendations from other producers.
- **Test and compare:** If possible, test out the equipment you are considering purchasing. Listen to the same track on multiple monitors or headphones to compare the sound quality.
- **Consider the environment:** Consider the acoustics of your studio environment when selecting gear. The gear you select should work well with the room's acoustic properties and help you achieve optimal sound quality.
- **Upgrade gradually:** If you are working with a limited budget, it's okay to upgrade gradually. Start with the essentials, such as a good microphone and audio interface, and gradually upgrade your gear over time.

The right equipment can help you achieve a more polished and professional sound, while lower quality equipment can result in a weaker and less defined sound. When selecting gear, it's essential to consider your needs, budget, and studio environment. Remember to research and test the gear before making a purchase and consider upgrading gradually if necessary.

How to Set up Your Own Professional Studio

Setting up a professional music production studio can seem like a daunting task, but with the right guidance and tools, it is entirely achievable. Let's take a look at a step-by-step guide for setting up your own professional studio.

Step 1: Choose Your Room

Consider the size of the room, the layout, the acoustics, and the amount of soundproofing required. You can choose to set up your studio in a spare room in your home, rent a commercial space, or build a standalone structure. Ensure that the room is large enough to accommodate all the necessary equipment, as well as the proper sound treatment.

Step 2: Invest in Equipment

The next step is to invest in high-quality equipment. A good studio setup requires a range of equipment, including a computer, DAW software, studio monitors, headphones, microphones, cables, and a mixer. Consider your budget and research the best equipment within your price range. It is essential to invest in high-quality equipment to ensure that your recordings sound professional.

Step 3: Make Provisions for Acoustic Treatment

Acoustic treatment is crucial to achieving optimal sound quality in a recording studio. Acoustic treatment involves the placement of sound-absorbing and diffusing materials to manage the sound waves within the room. This can include things like diffusers, bass traps, and even acoustic panels. To achieve optimal acoustics, consider hiring an acoustician or consulting online resources to ensure that your studio space is appropriately treated.

Step 4: Set up Your Equipment

Once you have your equipment and acoustic treatment sorted, the next step is to set up your equipment. Start by positioning your studio monitors at ear level and ensuring that they are positioned correctly to minimize reflections. Position your microphone stand and ensure that the microphone is positioned appropriately for recording. Connect your equipment and test your setup to ensure that everything is working correctly.

Step 5: Conduct Your Calibration

Calibrating your studio monitors is critical to achieving accurate sound reproduction. Use a reference track to adjust the settings on your monitors, in order to ensure that the sound is balanced across all frequencies. This step is essential to ensure that your recordings sound great across a range of playback systems.

Step 6: Get to Work

With your studio set up and calibrated, it's time to start creating music. Experiment with different sounds, techniques, and equipment to develop your unique sound. Don't be afraid to make mistakes and try new things; this is how you will develop your style and refine your production skills.

Setting up a professional music production studio requires a significant investment of time and money, but it is entirely achievable. Choose your space, invest in high-quality equipment, treat the acoustics, set up your equipment, calibrate your monitors, and get to work. With careful planning and attention to detail, you can create a professional studio that will allow you to produce high-quality music recordings. Remember that every studio is unique, and it may take some experimentation to find the setup that works best for your specific needs.

Studio Management and Organization

Studio management and organization are essential aspects of running a successful music production studio. The organization of your studio can impact your workflow, creativity, and productivity. An organized studio allows you to easily find the equipment and tools you need, reduces clutter and distractions, and helps you stay focused on the task at hand. A well-managed studio also helps you meet deadlines, stay on budget, and deliver high-quality work.

Tips for Studio Management and Organization

Here is how you can improve your studio management and organization:

- **Develop a system:** Organize your equipment and tools by creating a labeled storage system, grouping similar items together, and creating a checklist to ensure that all equipment is accounted for after each use.
- **Keep your studio clean:** Keeping your studio clean and free of clutter can help you stay organized and focused. Regularly clean and organize your equipment and workspaces, and establish a routine to maintain a clean environment.

- **Label everything:** Labeling your equipment and tools can make it easier to find what you need quickly. Consider labeling cables, equipment, and storage containers, and make sure that everyone in the studio follows the labeling system.
- **Establish a routine:** Establishing a routine can help you stay on task and ensure that your studio is always organized and ready for work. This can include scheduling regular maintenance and cleaning, setting aside time for paperwork and administrative tasks, and establishing a system for inventory management.
- **Invest in storage solutions:** Investing shelves, racks, and drawers can help you keep your studio organized and clutter-free. Consider investing in high-quality storage solutions that are durable and can hold all of your equipment and tools.
- **Develop a file management system:** Develop a file management system for your digital files, such as music files, sample libraries, and project files. Consider using a consistent naming convention and folder structure to make it easy to find and access files.
- **Train your team:** If you work with a team, make sure that everyone is trained to implement your studio management and organization system. Establish a training program to ensure that everyone understands the system and follows it consistently.

Effective studio management and organization takes time and effort, but the benefits are worth it. After enough time, it will become a habit, and you'll barely notice you are even doing it!

Working With Clients and Artists

Working with clients and artists is an essential part of being a music producer. Whether you are producing music for a commercial project, a film score, or working with an artist to create their album, effective communication and collaboration are key to producing high-quality work. In this section, we will discuss the importance of working with clients and artists, offer some tips for effective communication and collaboration, and explain some common challenges that may arise. Satisfied clients and artists can lead to future work and referrals, which can be valuable for growing your business or career.

Tips for Effective Communication and Collaboration

Communication is extremely important for your success as a music producer, but the skills needed to be effective in it don't always come naturally. Let's take a look at how you can develop good communication skills to ensure your collaborations always go well:

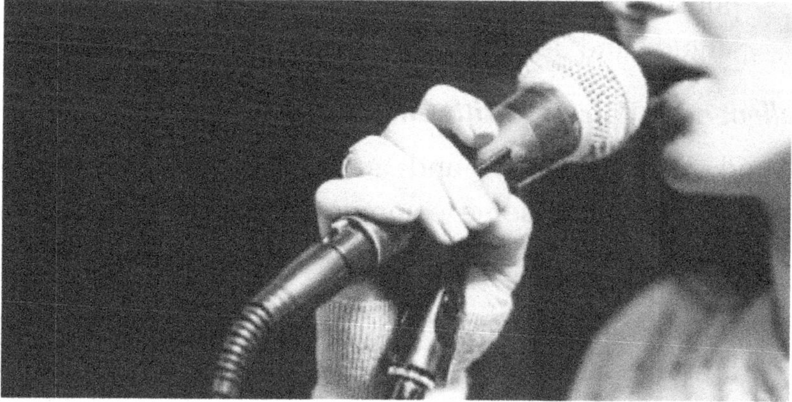

- **Set expectations:** At the beginning of the project, set expectations with your client or artist. This can include deadlines, budget, and the scope of the project. Make sure that everyone involved is on the same page to avoid misunderstandings or miscommunications down the line.

- **Listen and communicate:** Take the time to understand your client's or artist's vision and goals, and communicate clearly and honestly throughout the process.
- **Be flexible:** Flexibility is important when working with clients and artists, as their vision or goals may change throughout the project. Be open to making changes and adjustments, and communicate any potential issue or concern in a timely manner.
- **Establish boundaries**: It is important to establish boundaries with clients and artists to maintain a healthy and productive working relationship. Make sure that everyone involved understands their roles and responsibilities, and establish clear communication channels and working hours.
- **Be professional:** Professionalism is important when working with clients and artists. This includes being punctual, respecting deadlines, and maintaining a positive attitude and demeanor even in difficult situations.

Challenges of Working With Clients and Artists

Working with clients and artists can also present some challenges. Here are some common challenges that may arise and how to address them:

- **Creative differences:** These can arise when the client or artist has a different vision or goal for the project than you do. It is important to communicate effectively and find a solution that meets both parties' needs.
- **Budget and time constraints:** This can be challenging when working on a project. Be transparent with your client

or artist about any potential issue, and work together to find a solution that meets their needs while staying within the constraints.

- **Communication breakdowns:** These can occur when there is a lack of clarity or understanding between you and your client or artist. Make sure to communicate clearly and consistently, and establish a system for regular check-ins and updates.
- **Managing expectations:** This can be challenging when working with clients and artists. Make sure to set realistic expectations and communicate any potential issue or delay in a timely manner.

By setting expectations, listening and communicating effectively, being flexible, establishing boundaries, and maintaining professionalism, you can build positive relationships and establish a great reputation in the industry. Remember that challenges may arise when working with clients and artists, but with effective communication and problem-solving skills, you can overcome them and produce high quality productions.

CHAPTER 4
PRE-PRODUCTION AND RECORDING

In this chapter, we will take a closer look at the process of pre-production and recording.

Pre-Production

Pre-production is a vital stage in music production that sets the foundation for a successful project. The pre-production phase is where ideas are refined, creative goals are established, and technical issues are resolved. There are some reasons that explain why pre-production is important. These include the following:

- Pre-production can save you both time and money. By identifying and resolving issues before recording begins, you can prevent costly mistakes during the recording process. This includes identifying issues with the arrangement, tempo, or key of the song. Technical issues with equipment or instruments can also be resolved before recording begins, which can save valuable studio time.
- Pre-production provides an opportunity to clarify the vision for the project. This is essential for ensuring that everyone involved in the project is on the same page. By discussing the overall sound, desired mood or atmosphere, and any specific production techniques or effects, the artist and producer can establish a shared understanding of

what they are working towards.

- Pre-production is a great opportunity to work on the arrangement of the song. This involves editing or rearranging the structure of the song to ensure that it flows well and has a cohesive structure. By doing this, the producer can help to highlight the song's strengths and ensure that the arrangement is engaging and memorable.
- Pre-production allows for experimentation with different sounds, ideas, and techniques without the pressure of recording or tracking. This can include testing out different instruments, effects, or production techniques to see what works best for the song. By experimenting in the pre-production phase, the artist and producer can be more confident in their choices during the recording process.
- Pre-production provides an opportunity for the artist and producer to build a stronger relationship and develop a deeper understanding of each other's creative vision and goals for the project. This is essential for creating a comfortable and collaborative environment in the studio. By building trust and understanding between the artist and producer, the recording process can be more efficient and productive.

Pre-Production Steps

Here are some key steps that you can follow to create an effective pre-production process:

1. **Discuss and clarify the vision:** The first step in pre-production is to discuss and clarify the vision for the project. This involves having a conversation with the artist or band to understand their creative vision and goals for the project. It is essential to determine the overall sound,

the desired mood or atmosphere, and any specific production technique or effect that will be used.

2. **Work on the arrangement:** Once the vision has been established, the next step is to work on the arrangement of the song. This can involve editing or rearranging the structure of the song to ensure that it flows well and has a cohesive structure. It is also essential to determine the tempo and key of the song during this stage.
3. **Experiment with sounds and ideas:** Pre-production provides an opportunity to experiment with different sounds, ideas, and techniques without the pressure of recording or tracking. This can include testing out different instruments, effects, or production techniques to see what works best for the song. The experimentation can lead to discovering new creative ideas that can enhance the production quality of the final product.
4. **Identify technical issues:** During pre-production, it is essential to identify and resolve any technical issue with equipment or instruments. This can include testing microphones, checking cables and connections, and troubleshooting any issues that arise. It is better to address technical issues in the pre-production stage to avoid disruptions during the actual recording session.
5. **Set goals and deadlines:** Finally, it's important to set goals and deadlines for the project during pre-production. This can help to ensure that everyone involved is on the same page and that the project stays on track. It is crucial to set a realistic timeline to allow sufficient time for recording, mixing, and mastering.

Recording

In this section, we will take a look at the recording process, from the different kinds of microphones available to tips on recording vocals, as well as different kinds of instruments.

Types of Microphones and Their Uses

In music production, microphones play a crucial role in capturing the sound of instruments and vocals. There are several types of microphones available, each with its own characteristics and uses. Understanding the different types of microphones and their applications can help producers and engineers to achieve the desired sound in their recordings. The different types of microphones include:

- **Dynamic microphones:** These are durable and versatile microphones, making them a popular choice for live performances and for recording instruments such as drums and electric guitars. They work by using a moving coil attached to a diaphragm, which creates a magnetic field that converts sound waves into electrical signals. Dynamic microphones are relatively inexpensive and have a high resistance to handling noise, making them an ideal choice for recording loud instruments.

ribbon microphone

dynamic microphone

condenser microphone

- **Condenser microphones:** These microphones are more sensitive and responsive than dynamic microphones, making them an excellent choice for recording vocals and acoustic instruments. They work by using a thin diaphragm that vibrates in response to sound waves, creating an electrical signal. Condenser microphones require phantom power, which is typically provided by a mixing console or external power supply. They are also more fragile than dynamic microphones and require careful handling.
- **Ribbon microphones:** These are known for their warm and natural sound, making them a popular choice for recording instruments such as strings and horns. They work by using a thin ribbon of metal suspended between two magnets, which vibrates in response to sound waves. Ribbon microphones are highly sensitive and have a figure-eight polar pattern, which means they pick up sound from the front and back but not from the sides.
- **Shotgun microphones:** These are highly directional microphones and are commonly used in film and television production to capture dialogue and sound effects. They work by using a long, narrow tube that captures sound from a specific direction while minimizing background noise. Shotgun microphones are ideal for recording in noisy environments and can be used to capture sound from a distance.
- **Boundary microphones:** These are designed to be placed on a surface, such as a table or floor, and are ideal for recording meetings, lectures, and other events. They work by using a flat diaphragm that captures sound waves as they bounce off the surface. Boundary microphones have

a wide pickup pattern and are ideal for capturing sound in large rooms.

- **Wireless microphones:** These are ideal for performers who need to move around the stage during a live performance. They work by conveying sound from a transmitter which is connected to the microphone and sends a signal to a receiver which, in turn, is typically connected to a mixing console or amplifier. Wireless microphones can be either dynamic or condenser and are available in handheld, lapel, and headset styles.

The type of microphone you use in your music production will depend on the specific application and desired sound.

Tips for Recording Vocals, Guitars, Drums, and Other Instruments

Recording instruments and vocals is a crucial part of music production. Whether you're a beginner or an experienced producer, there are always tips and tricks to improve your recordings. Let's explore some essential tips for recording vocals, guitars, drums, and other instruments.

Recording Vocals

1. **Choose the right microphone:** The microphone you choose can have a significant impact on the final recording. A large-diaphragm condenser microphone is a popular choice for recording vocals, as it can capture the nuances of the performance and provide a warm sound.
2. **Find the sweet spot:** This is the position where the microphone captures the best sound. Experiment with microphone placement and listen carefully to find the sweet spot for the vocalist's voice.
3. **Control the room acoustics:** The room you record in can have a significant impact on the sound of the recording. A vocal booth or a reflection filter can also help to isolate the vocals from the rest of the room.
4. **Use a pop filter:** This is a small device that is placed between the vocalist and the microphone. It helps to reduce plosives and other unwanted sounds that can be caused by fast-moving air, such as when pronouncing words with "p" or "b" sounds.
5. **Monitor the recording:** Make sure to monitor the recording closely as you go. Pay attention to the performance and adjust the microphone placement or other settings as necessary.

Recording Guitars

1. **Choose the right microphone:** There are several types of microphones that can be used to record guitars, including dynamic, condenser, and ribbon microphones. Experiment with different microphone types and placements to find the sound that works best for the guitar and the song.
2. **Control the room acoustics:** As with recording vocals, the room you record in can have a significant impact on the sound of the recording. A guitar amp isolation box can also help to isolate the guitar sound from the rest of the room.
3. **Experiment with microphone placement:** The placement of the microphone can have a significant impact on the sound of the recording. Experiment with different placements, such as close-miking the guitar amp, using a room mic, or a combination of both.
4. **Use a DI box:** This can be used to capture the direct signal from an electric guitar or bass and can be useful for creating a clean sound or for processing the signal later.
5. **Monitor the recording:** As with recording vocals, it's important to monitor the recording closely as you go. Pay attention to the performance and adjust the microphone

placement or other settings as necessary.

Recording Drums

1. **Choose the right microphone:** There are several types of microphones that can be used to record drums, including dynamic, condenser, and ribbon microphones. Experiment with different microphone types and placements to find the sound that works best for the drums and the song.
2. **Control the room acoustics:** As with recording vocals and guitars, the room you record drums in can have a significant impact on the sound of the recording. A drum enclosure or a drum booth can also help to isolate the drum sound from the rest of the room.
3. **Use multiple microphones:** Recording drums often requires the use of multiple microphones to capture the different elements of the drum kit. Experiment with different microphone placements, such as close-miking the individual drums and cymbals, using overhead or room microphones, or a combination of both.
4. **Position the microphones correctly:** The positioning of the microphones is critical when recording drums. The

placement of the microphone can have a significant impact on the sound of the drums. Experiment with different positions and determine which is the best.

5. **Use proper drum tuning:** It is essential to tune the drums correctly before recording. A well-tuned drum can provide a better tone and sustain the overall sound quality. Tune the drums in a way that complements the music genre and style you are recording.
6. **Control the room sound:** This is important when recording drums. You want to capture the sound of the drums, not the room's reverberation. Consider using acoustic panels, blankets, or other sound-absorbing materials to minimize the room's reflections.

Tips for Recording Other Instruments

1. **Select the right microphone:** Each instrument has unique sound characteristics, and therefore requires a specific type of microphone. Choose a microphone that complements the instrument's sound qualities and provides the desired tone.
2. **Position the microphone correctly:** Proper microphone placement is critical when recording instruments. The placement can affect the sound quality and tone of the instrument. Experiment with different positions and angles to find the best spot.
3. **Eliminate background noise:** Background noise can be distracting and affect the overall sound quality of the recording. Eliminate any unnecessary noise source like fans, air conditioners, or other instruments.
4. **Control the room sound:** The sound of the room can impact the recorded instrument's tone and quality. Consider using sound-absorbing materials like acoustic

panels, blankets, or rugs to control the room's sound and minimize reflections.

Recording instruments and vocals requires careful planning, preparation, and attention to detail. By following the tips outlined above, you can create high-quality recordings that capture the essence of your music. Remember to experiment, be patient, and trust your ears to achieve the best results. With the right approach and techniques, you can achieve professional-quality recordings that showcase your musical talents.

Recording Techniques and Best Practices

Recording techniques and best practices are essential to ensure that a music production project achieves the desired sound and quality. Whether you are recording in a professional studio or a home setup, there are several techniques and practices that can help you achieve optimal results. Let's discuss some key recording techniques and best practices to help you produce high-quality recordings.

Mic Placement

Mic placement is crucial to achieving the desired sound and can significantly affect the tone and quality of the recording.

Experimenting with different mic positions can help you achieve the best sound for the instrument or voice being recorded. For example, during the process of recording vocals, the mic should be placed at a comfortable distance from the singer's mouth to avoid pops and sibilance. For guitar or bass recording, the mic can be placed close to the speaker or further away, depending on the desired tone.

Gain Staging

Proper gain staging is crucial to achieving a clean and balanced mix. Gain staging refers to the process of optimizing the gain (volume) of each component in the recording chain to ensure a balanced signal level. This can be achieved by adjusting the gain of the microphone preamp, compressor, and mixer to achieve optimal levels without introducing unwanted noise or distortion.

Room Acoustics

The acoustics of the recording room can have a significant impact on the overall sound quality. The ideal recording environment is a neutral space that is free from unwanted reflections or resonance. Consider using acoustic treatment, such as absorptive panels or diffusers, to optimize the recording environment and minimize unwanted sound reflections.

Editing

Editing is an essential part of the recording process. Proper editing can help you achieve a clean and polished sound by removing unwanted noise, clicks, pops, or other imperfections. Consider using a software editor such as Pro Tools or Logic to edit and mix your recordings.

Monitoring

Monitoring is the process of listening to the recording while it is being made to ensure that the sound is captured correctly. Good monitoring is crucial to achieving the best possible sound. Consider using high-quality headphones or studio monitors to ensure accurate sound reproduction and to monitor the recording for any issue or problem that may need to be addressed.

Multiple Recordings

Taking multiple recordings is a good practice that can help you achieve the best possible sound. Recording multiple takes of a track can help you capture different nuances and variations in the performance, giving you more options to choose from during the mixing stage. This can help you achieve a more dynamic and interesting mix.

High-Quality Equipment

High-quality equipment can make a significant difference in the quality of the recording. Using high-quality microphones, preamps, and other equipment can help you achieve a clean and professional sound. However, keep in mind that high-quality equipment does not necessarily guarantee good recordings. Proper technique and knowledge are also crucial to achieving optimal results. It's also important to note that high price does not mean high quality. Talk with peers in the same field, and look for reviews online to find out which equipment will give you the best results for your budget.

Professionals

If you are unsure of the recording techniques or best practices, consider working with a professional recording engineer. A professional engineer can help you achieve the best possible sound and provide valuable guidance and advice.

Common Recording Mistakes to Avoid

While there is no one-size-fits-all approach to recording, there are some common mistakes that musicians and engineers should avoid to ensure a successful recording session. Let's take a look at some of these mistakes and tips on how you can avoid them.

Not Preparing Enough

One of the most common mistakes in recording is not preparing enough. This can include not tuning instruments or not practicing enough before the recording session. It's important to make sure that all instruments are in tune and that the musicians are comfortable playing their parts before hitting the record button.

Not Using Proper Microphone Placement

Microphone placement is crucial in recording. Placing a microphone too close to an instrument or amplifier can result in distortion or unwanted noise, while placing it too far away can result in a weak signal. It's important to experiment with different microphone placements to find the sweet spot for each instrument.

Not Checking Levels

Setting levels properly is essential for a clean and professional-sounding recording. Recording at levels that are too high can result in distortion, while recording at levels that are too low can result in a weak signal that requires amplification in post-production. It's important to check levels regularly during recording to ensure that they are consistent and appropriate for each instrument and voice.

Not Using Headphones

Wearing headphones during recording allows musicians to hear their own playing and the other musicians in the mix. This can help with timing, pitch, and overall cohesion of the performance. It's important to make sure that the headphones are comfortable and that the mix is balanced to avoid fatigue or hearing damage.

Not Taking Breaks

Recording can be a tiring and intense process, and it's important to take breaks to avoid fatigue and burnout. Taking breaks allows musicians to rest their ears and their minds, which can improve the overall quality of the recording. It's important to schedule regular breaks throughout the recording session to take time to relax and recharge.

Not Editing Properly

Editing is an important part of the recording process, but it's important to use it wisely. Over-editing can result in a sterile and unnatural sound, while under-editing can result in a sloppy and unprofessional recording. It's important to strike a balance between editing out mistakes and preserving the natural energy and emotion of the performance.

Not Backing up Files

Recording sessions can be unpredictable, and technical issues can arise at any time. It's important to back up all files regularly to avoid losing important data. This can include backing up files to an external hard drive, cloud storage, or other reliable backup solutions.

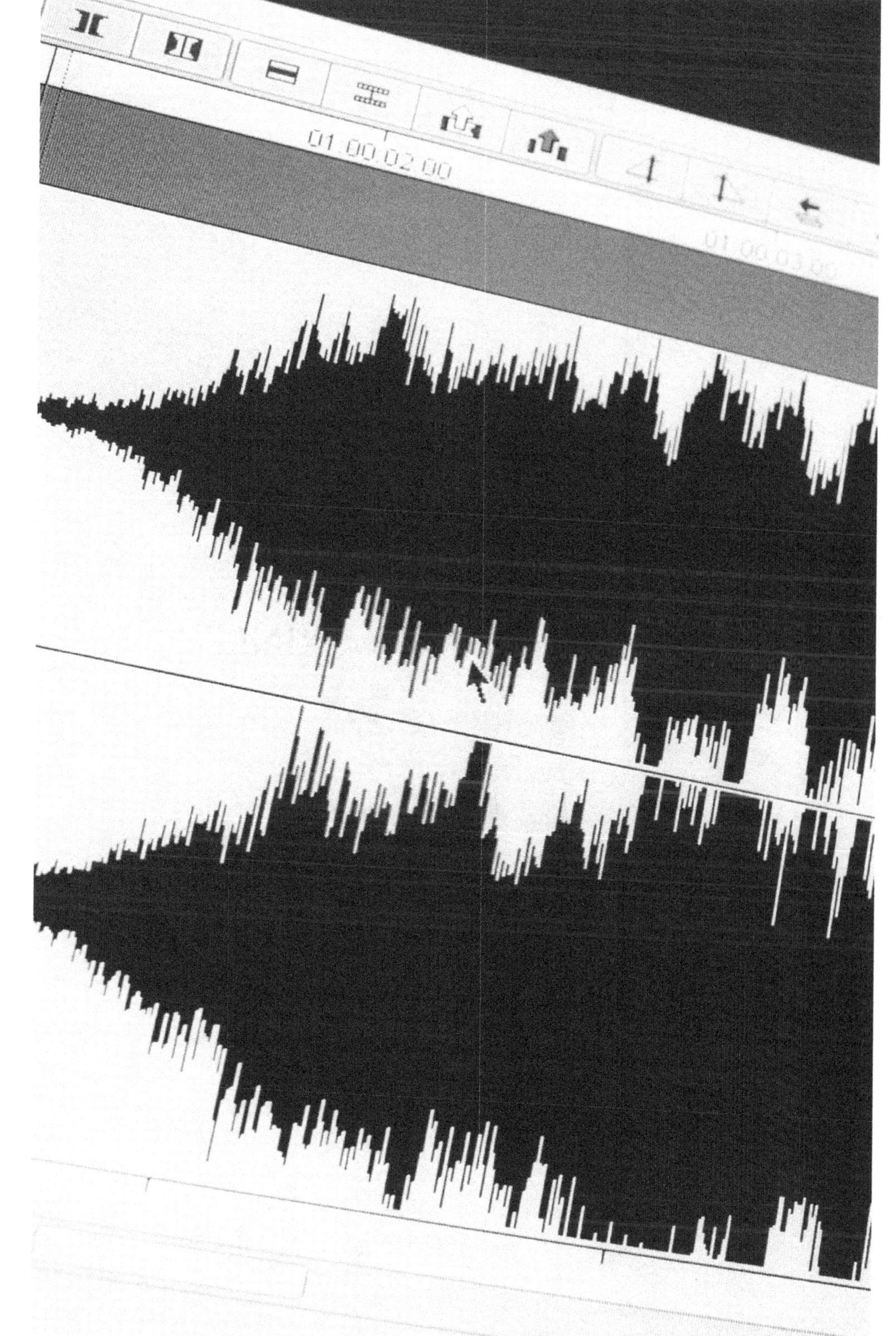
01.00.02.00
01.00.03.00

CHAPTER 5
EDITING AND MIXING

Editing involves manipulating the audio recordings to enhance their quality and coherence. Mixing is a system of adjusting and balancing the various elements of a song to achieve a quality result. These two processes are essential in making a track sound professional and ready for release. In this chapter, we will explore the fundamentals of editing and mixing, including techniques for adjusting volume, EQ, compression, and other effects, as well as the tools used in the process. We will also cover some best practices for editing audio to improve its quality and flow, and also techniques for achieving a well-balanced mix. Understanding these essential elements of music production will take your tracks to the next level.

Editing Techniques for Improving the Overall Sound Quality of Recordings

Recording audio is only the beginning of the process when it comes to music production. The next step is editing the recordings to ensure they have the best possible sound quality. While there are many editing techniques available, some of the most effective are noise reduction, equalization, compression, and volume adjustment.

Noise Reduction

Noise can be a major issue for audio recordings, and it can come from many different sources. Electrical interference is a common culprit, especially when recording with unshielded cables or in areas with a lot of electrical equipment. Background noise can also be a problem, whether it's the sound of traffic outside, people talking in another room, or even the sound of the air-conditioning or heating system. Some equipment can even introduce noise, such as hiss from an amplifier or the hum of a microphone, into the recording itself.

Fortunately, there are tools available to help reduce or eliminate unwanted noise from your recordings. One such tool is a noise gate. A noise gate is a type of audio processing that allows you to set a threshold level below which any incoming sound is muted. This means that, during quiet parts of a recording, any background noise will be silenced. For example, if you're recording a voiceover and there's a lot of traffic outside, you can set the noise gate to only allow audio above a certain level, effectively muting any background noise. Noise gates can be especially useful for reducing the sound of hums and buzzes from equipment.

Another tool for reducing noise in audio recordings is a noise reduction plugin. They can be particularly useful for removing constant background noise, such as the hum of a refrigerator or the sound of a fan. Most noise reduction plugins work by analyzing a section of audio that contains only the noise, then using that information to filter out the noise from the rest of the recording. It's important to note that noise reduction plugins can sometimes affect the quality of the audio, so it's best to use them sparingly and only when necessary.

There are a few other techniques for reducing noise in audio recordings. For example, placing a microphone closer to the sound source can help reduce the amount of background noise picked up. Using a pop filter can also help reduce unwanted noise, especially when recording vocals. Choose a recording environment that is as quiet as possible, with minimal background noise or interference.

Equalization

You might be familiar with using an equalization (EQ) on your phone or radio, but most people don't really understand how it works. EQ is a critical tool in the process of audio mixing and editing. It allows you to adjust the balance of frequencies in a recording to achieve a more polished, professional sound. Essentially, EQ is about making sure that every element of the mix has its own space and isn't fighting for attention with other elements.

EQ works by dividing the audio spectrum into different frequency ranges, and allowing you to adjust the volume of each range. These frequency ranges are commonly referred to as bands. For example, you might have a low-frequency band that covers everything below 100 Hz, a mid-range band that covers frequencies from 500 Hz to 2 kHz, and a high-frequency band that covers everything above 8 kHz. You can adjust the volume of each of these bands individually to create a more balanced sound.

One common use of EQ is to fix problems in a recording. For example, if a recording sounds muddy or lacking in clarity, you can use EQ to boost the higher frequencies to bring out the details. Conversely, if a recording sounds too bright or harsh, you can cut the higher frequencies to tame the sound. EQ can also be used to create separation between different elements of the mix. For example, if you have a guitar and a piano playing at the same time, you might use EQ to boost the high frequencies of the guitar and cut the high frequencies of the piano, so that each instrument has its own space in the mix.

However, it's important to use EQ sparingly and judiciously, as too much boosting or cutting can create an unnatural or unbalanced sound. It's best to start with small adjustments and listen carefully to the effect they have on the overall sound. You can also use visual EQ displays to help you see where the problem frequencies are, and where adjustments might be needed.

Compression

Compression is a technique used to even out the dynamic range of a recording, making the quiet parts louder and the loud parts quieter. This can create a more consistent and polished sound. Compression works by reducing the level of any audio signal that exceeds a certain threshold. This can be especially useful for vocal recordings, as it can help even out any variations in volume or intensity. A music producer can use compression in many ways to enhance the sound of a recording.

A producer can also use compression to control the dynamics of a recording by reducing the volume of the loudest parts and increasing the volume of the quietest parts. This can make the recording sound more even and consistent. For example, if a recording has a loud guitar solo that is overpowering the rest of the instruments, the producer can use compression to reduce the volume of the guitar solo and bring it in line with the rest of the mix.

Compression can also be used to emphasize or de-emphasize certain elements of a mix. For example, if the drums are an important element of the mix, the producer can use compression to make them sound punchier and more prominent. On the other hand, if there is a background instrument that is getting lost in the mix, the producer can use compression to bring it forward.

It can also be used to add sustain to an instrument. This can be especially useful for guitar solos or other lead instruments. By compressing the signal, the sustain of the notes is increased, making them sound longer and more expressive.

Compression is especially useful for controlling the dynamics of a vocal recording. By using compression, the producer can even out the volume of the vocals, making them sound more consistent and polished. This is important for ensuring that the vocals are always audible and that the listener doesn't have to strain to hear them. Compression can also be used to create a sense of space in a mix. By compressing the reverb or delay effect, the producer can make the sound appear to be farther away, creating a sense of depth in the mix.

Volume Adjustment

Volume adjustment is a simple but important technique for improving the overall sound quality of a recording. It involves adjusting the volume level of individual tracks to create a more balanced mix. This also enables you to reduce the volume of certain tracks that are overpowering others, and to boost the volume of quieter tracks that need to be heard more clearly. It's important to be careful not to overdo volume adjustments, as too much boosting can lead to distortion and clipping.

By using these methods in combination, you can create a polished, professional sound that will make your recordings stand out. Remember to use these techniques sparingly, as overuse can create an unnatural or unbalanced sound. With practice and experimentation, you'll soon be able to master these techniques.

Basic Mixing Concepts and Techniques

Mixing is the process of combining multiple audio tracks into a cohesive final product. It involves adjusting the volume, panning, EQ, compression, and other effects to create a balanced and polished sound. There are certain basic mixing concepts and techniques that every music producer should be familiar with.

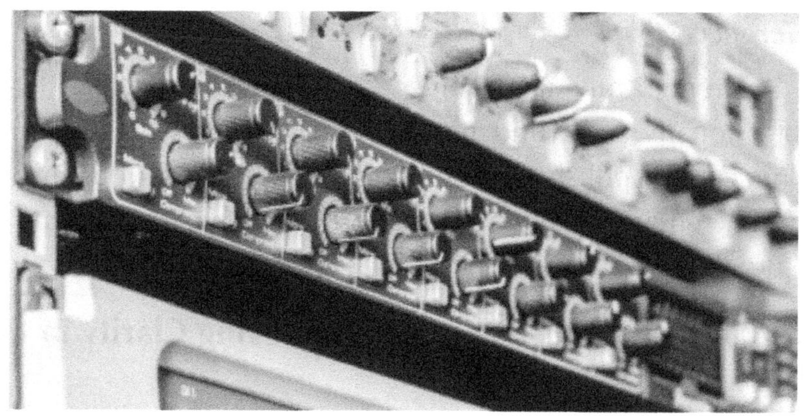

Gain Staging

Gain staging is the process of setting the levels of each track to ensure that they are consistent and not clipping or distorting. It's important to set the levels of each track so that they have enough headroom for processing or effects that will be added later in the mix.

Panning

Panning refers to the placement of each track in the stereo field. By panning tracks to the left or right, you can achieve a feeling of depth and space in the mix. It's important to consider the role of each track in the mix and place them accordingly. For example, the kick drum and bass guitar may be panned center, while the rhythm guitar and keyboard are panned slightly to the left and right.

Effects

Effects such as reverb, delay, and chorus can add depth and character to a mix. It's important to use effects tastefully and consider the role of each track in the mix. For example, a guitar solo may benefit from a long reverb to create a sense of space, while the vocals may benefit from a subtle delay to add depth.

Reference Mixing

Reference mixing involves comparing your mix to a professionally mixed and mastered track to ensure that it sounds balanced and polished. It's important to listen to your mix in different environments and on different playback systems to ensure that it translates well.

Creating a Balanced Mix and Achieving Clarity in the Mix

Creating a balanced mix with clarity is a critical aspect of music production. A balanced mix refers to having all the elements of a track sound equally audible and present in the mix. Clarity refers to being able to hear each individual sound clearly, without any muddiness or distortion. Here are some tips to achieve a balanced mix with clarity:

- **Use panning and stereo imaging:** These are powerful tools that are used to create separation between instruments and make sure that they don't clash with each other. Use panning to position each instrument in the stereo field and create a sense of space. Use stereo imaging to enhance the stereo width of specific tracks, such as the drums or the guitar.
- **Pay attention to levels:** Making sure that each track is at the appropriate level is crucial in achieving a balanced mix. Make sure that no instrument is too loud or too soft relative to the rest of the mix. Use volume faders to adjust the levels of each track and create a consistent balance.
- **Use EQ to create space:** As mentioned earlier, EQ is an essential tool to create separation between tracks. Use EQ to cut or boost specific frequencies to create space

for each instrument. For example, cutting some low frequencies from the bass guitar can create more room for the kick drum in the low end.

- **Avoid frequency masking:** This occurs when two or more instruments occupy the same frequency range and clash with each other. Use EQ to create separation and avoid frequency masking. You can also use sidechain compression to duck the level of a track when another track is playing in the same frequency range.
- **Use compression and limiting:** These are powerful tools that are used to even out the dynamic range of a mix and make it sound more polished. Use compression to control the dynamics of individual tracks, and use limiting to prevent clipping and ensure that the mix doesn't get too loud.
- **Use reference tracks:** Referencing your mix against professional, well-mixed tracks can help you achieve a balanced mix with clarity. Listen to how other mixes sound and try to emulate the balance and clarity in your own mix.

Now that you have a basic understanding of the mixing and editing stage of music production, let's take a look at some more advanced techniques in the next chapter.

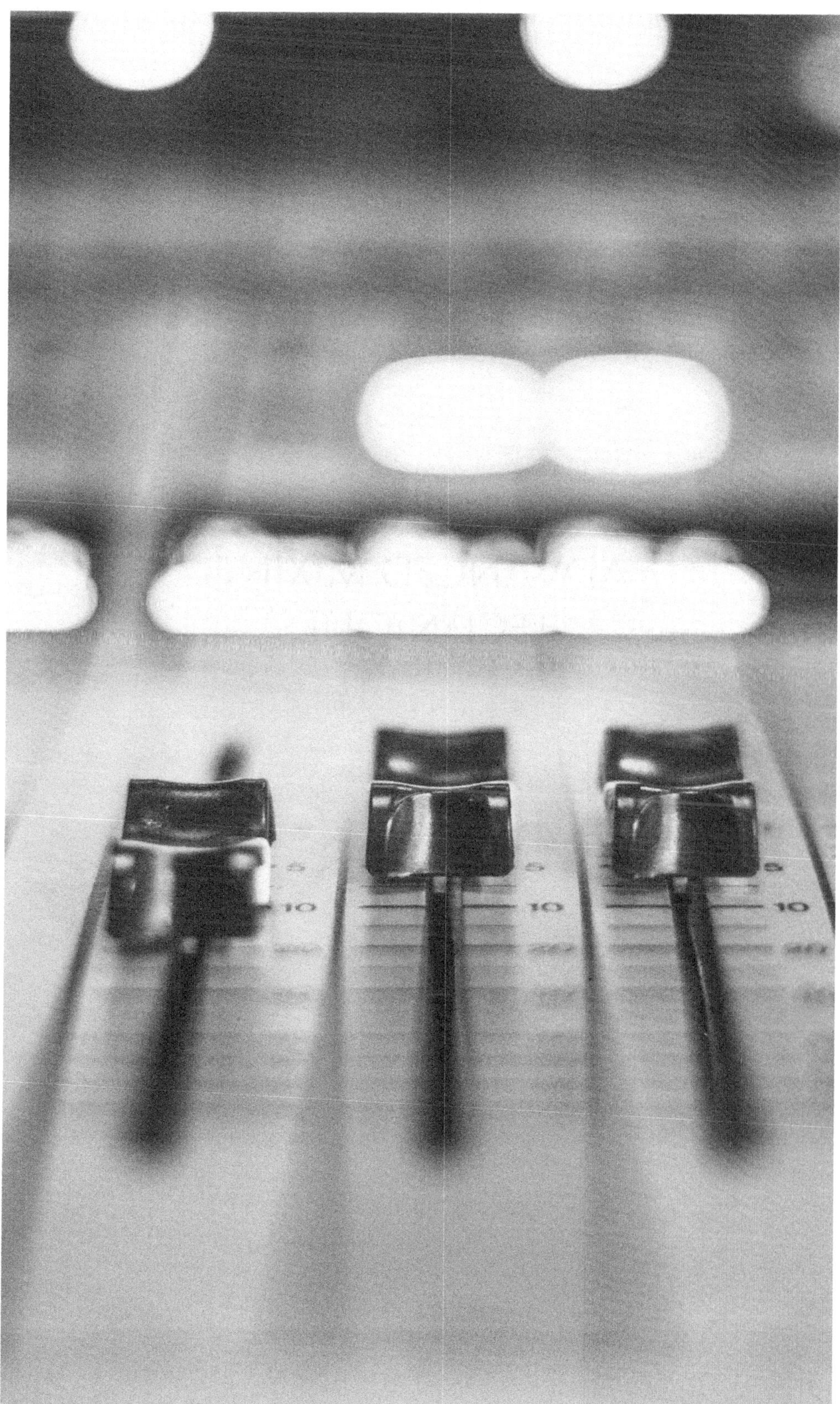

CHAPTER 6
ADVANCED MIXING TECHNIQUES

Advanced mixing techniques in music production can help you to create a polished and professional sound. Here are some that can help you achieve a more complex and nuanced mix.

Multiband Compression

Multiband compression is a tool that allows you to compress specific frequency ranges. This technique can be especially useful for controlling the dynamics of specific instruments or sounds that occupy a specific frequency range. Multiband compression is similar to a combination of an EQ and a compressor. It allows you to compress specific frequency ranges separately, making it possible to achieve more nuanced compression. For example, you can heavily compress the high-end to above 10 kHz while leaving the low end more subtly compressed.

Multiband compression can be used to deal with inconsistencies in tone, as narrow or wide band frequencies can have varied dynamics, while the rest of the sound remains unvaried. Even though this could also be achieved by using a normal compressor, a multiband compressor is recommended for precision.

A portion of the frequency range can be taken and compressed as a distinct source with multiband compression, leaving the rest of the sound unaffected. This makes it sound transparent and more natural.

Because the adjustment is static, using an EQ to lower a particular frequency band might not be as successful as it could be. When you turn down a frequency range with EQ, it is always turned down by the same amount, regardless of the loudness of the sound.

Multiband compression, on the contrary, only reduces a particular frequency range when it is loud, otherwise leaving it unaltered. This makes it a good tool for addressing tonal inconsistencies without affecting the overall balance of the sound.

Before you start using multiband compression, you should understand that EQ and compression should always be your first line of defense when it comes to tonal issues. Most of the time, your mix problems can be rectified by using only these two tools.

However, if you're still struggling to solve the issue, then it may be time to turn to a multiband compressor. This tool allows you to combine EQ and compression into one interface, making it easier to target specific frequency ranges and apply nuanced compression.

Multiband compression has two key components: bands and compression settings. A large range of frequencies can be processed using bands, which are similar to broad EQ curves. The bands are divided up next to one another, and the crossover frequency determines how they interact. Depending on your preferences, you can select a certain frequency point and either a steep or gradual curve in some multiband compressors. Steep curves are more exact, but gradual curves will appear more natural.

Once you've selected a band, you'll have access to a set of compression settings, which may include

- Ratio
- Threshold
- Attack & Release
- Knee
- Range
- Lookahead
- Dry/Wet

Each band will have its own unique set of controls, except for Dry/Wet, which is usually universal.

Now that you have a grasp of multiband compressors, let's discuss when and how to use them effectively.

Here are a variety of ways that multiband compression can be helpful:

- **Tonal inconsistency balance:** If you have a problem with a particular frequency range in your mix that a regular EQ cannot solve, you can use a multiband compressor. This is especially helpful when working with acoustic or organic sound sources, which typically have greater dynamics than synthesized or digital sounds. Examples of this are an acoustic guitar or a human voice. In your workflow, you can attempt to solve the issue with EQ first. If the problem persists, use a multiband compressor to target the problematic frequency range. Use a ratio of

4:1 (or thereabouts) and set the threshold to trigger when the inconsistency occurs. Adjust the attack and release to achieve a natural sound, depending on the material. Remember to adjust the ratio and threshold as needed to make the adjustments sound more transparent. A/B test the signal and use the Dry/Wet knob if the effect is too noticeable.

- **General dynamic control:** A multiband compressor can be used to balance and bind your mix so that it sounds broader. Make the compression specific to each band rather than using a general approach. For example, compress the high-end energy a lot but use a more subtle ratio on the mids and a higher ratio on the lows to tighten them up. In your workflow here, you can first attempt to control your mix with a compressor. Listen to the sections of the audio that would be affected by standard compression if the issue persists. It is best to process the bits that were not compressed first. You can then move on to less aggressive settings. Apply the appropriate amount to each band during the operation. Check the signal, and if the effect is too pronounced, use the Dry/Wet knob.
- **De-essing and de-popping:** A de-esser acts like a multiband compressor with more complex controls for a particular frequency range. De-popping is a comparable problem, except it occurs at the low end of the spectrum. To fix these problems, you can use a multiband compressor plugin or a conventional de-esser plugin. You can use the same procedure as the first workflow described above, but keep in mind that EQ might not be able to fix a very sibilant vocal without degrading the

audio as a whole.

- **Creative sound design:** You can use a multiband compressor creatively to achieve unique sound design. For instance, Live's Multiband Dynamics' OTT preset dramatically changes a sound's character by making it more crushed and thick. There is no fixed method for employing a multiband compressor in this manner, but you can play with presets, employ numerous instances, greatly compress the music by turning up the input gain, and adjust random settings.

Parallel Compression

A method of compression called parallel compression combines a signal that has been extensively compressed with the original, unprocessed signal. While retaining the original dynamics, this method can give a music additional sustain and presence. For instance, to make a lead vocal more noticeable in the mix, employ parallel compression.

Parallel compression is a type of upward compression that takes advantage of human hearing by boosting quieter parts of a performance while retaining its transients. This is possible because our ears are more sensitive to sudden reductions in volume of loud sounds than to increases in volume of quiet sounds. Unlike downward compression, which can reduce the intensity and feel of a performance, parallel compression preserves these qualities in a pleasing way and can make a track sound more aggressive and exciting.

To set up parallel compression, you need to route the signal in two directions, with one being heavily compressed and the other being the original audio. In an analog console, you would mix the two signals together by ear. In a DAW, you can create an auxiliary buss for the track you want to process and apply dramatic compression to it. When you are finished with these steps, the signals can be blended using the Send or duplicating the original.

When using parallel compression in a DAW, it's important to account for latency. Comb-filtering and phasing effects can be created when signals on parallel paths arrive at the mix buss at different times. This can be avoided by compressing the unprocessed signal using settings that are more moderate than the parallel signal. This ensures that both signals go through the same number of processing stages and are delayed by the same amount of time.

To get the "in-your-face" sound that parallel compression is known for, you need to set the compressor aggressively with low thresholds and high ratios for ample amounts of gain reduction. A fast attack and slower release both works well, but you should experiment with different settings since no two mixes are alike.

Stereo Widening

Stereo widening is used in audio production to make a stereo recording sound wider and more spacious. The basic principle behind stereo widening is to create a sense of separation between the left and right channels, making the mix appear wider than it actually is. There are several ways to achieve this, including:

- **EQ:** One simple way to create stereo width is to use an EQ to boost certain frequencies in one channel while reducing them in the other. For example, you could boost the high frequencies on the right channel while reducing them on the left, or vice versa.

- **Delay:** Another way to create stereo width is to introduce a slight delay between the left and right channels. This gives the two channels an impression of distance and separation. The delay time can be adjusted to taste, depending on how wide or narrow you want the mix to sound.
- **Reverb:** This can be used to add space and depth to a mix, and can also be used to create a sense of stereo width. By applying different amounts of reverb to the left and right channels, you can create a sense of separation between them.
- **Stereo imaging plugins:** There are a variety of plugins available that are specifically designed for stereo widening. These plugins work by manipulating the phase relationship between the left and right channels, creating a sense of space and separation between them.

It's worth noting that stereo widening is sometimes seen as both subjective and controversial for many artists, some like it while others don't. At the end of the day it's up to you to decide if you want to use it. Some engineers and producers prefer to keep their mixes relatively narrow, while others use stereo widening techniques to create a more expansive and immersive sound. As with any production techniques, the key is to use your ears and make creative choices that serve the needs of the song.

Mid-Side Processing

Manipulation of the stereo image occurs during mixing and mastering and is done using mid-side processing. This technique is based on the fact that every stereo recording has two main components: the center or mono signal, which is composed of sounds that are equal in both the left and right channels; and the side signal, which is composed of sounds that are different between the left and right channels.

The goal of mid-side processing is to separate these two components, so that you can apply different processing techniques to each one. For example, if you have a vocal track that is panned to the center of the mix, you may want to boost its volume and presence without affecting the rest of the mix. By using mid-side processing, you can boost the level of the center channel without affecting the sides, which could result in a clearer and more focused vocal sound.

To implement mid-side processing, you need a plugin or a processor that can split the stereo signal into two separate channels: the mid channel and the side channel. This can be done using a stereo imager plugin or a mid-side EQ. Once the stereo signal is split, you can apply different processing to each channel.

For example, to boost the center of the mix using mid-side processing, you would apply a boost to the mid channel while keeping the side channel relatively unaffected. To do this, insert a mid-side EQ on the track you want to process and select the mid channel. Then, boost the desired frequency range (such as the vocal range), while keeping the side channel flat or even attenuated. This will make the vocals stand out more in the mix without affecting the overall stereo width.

Mid-side processing can also be used when adjusting the stereo width of the track. For example, if a mix feels too narrow, you can widen it by applying a boost to the side channel while keeping the mid channel relatively unaffected. This will make the mix feel wider without changing the balance between the center and sides. To do this, insert a mid-side EQ on the track and select the side channel. Then, boost the desired frequency range, such as the high frequencies, while keeping the mid channel flat or even attenuated. This will create a wider stereo image while keeping the center of the mix intact.

Reverb

Reverb can help create the illusion of space and natural depth in your music. However, it can also be a bit tricky to master, especially if you're new to the process. Reverberation happens when sound waves reflect off surfaces inside of a space, producing a number of acoustic reflections.

Reverb is a type of effect that simulates these reflections and helps us create a sense of space and natural depth in our music. Whereas delay directly replicates a certain sound, reverb is achieved by a convergence of reflections and repetitions. As a result, a cohesive sound is produced.

A reverb signal typically consists of three components:

- The source signal refers to "the original dry sound source, which helps listeners identify where the sound is coming from" (Mastering the Mix, 2021).
- Early reflections occur when the sound source hits a wall or hard surface for the first time, typically within the first 30 ms of the sound occurring. These reflections help listeners identify their position within the room relative to the sound source.
- A decay tail is the sound that we hear as it bounces around the room, sort of like an echo. We hear more reverb and less direct signal as the sound reverberates in the room.

Music without reverb might sound artificial and flat. Reverb offers hints about the performance's setting and the locations of each instrument in the space. It can be compared to front-to-back pan controls for your mix, allowing you to control the balance between the center and sides of a mix.

Different Types of Reverb

Let's dive deeper into the different types of reverbs available to you as a mixing engineer. The type of reverb you choose can make a significant difference in the overall sound and feel of your mix. Listed below are the most commonly used reverb types:

- **Plate reverb:** Originally, metal plated were used to create this reverb and this is where the term originates from. Plate reverbs have a smooth and silky sound, making them perfect for vocals and drums. They are often used in vintage recordings and add a warm and spacious quality to a mix.
- **Spring reverb:** These reverbs were used in classic guitar amplifiers and are often associated with vintage rock and roll. They have a bright and lively sound with a quick decay time, making them perfect for adding a sense of space to guitar tracks.
- **Hall reverb:** This reverb type is used to add the sense of grandeur and space that are the characteristic of large concert halls. They have a long decay time and are perfect for orchestral recordings, choirs, and other large ensembles.
- **Room reverb:** In contrast to hall reverb, this technique emulates the sound quality of a small to medium sized room and the intimacy and warmth that characterize it. They have a shorter decay time than hall reverbs and are often used on acoustic instruments, such as guitars, pianos, and drums.
- **Chamber reverb:** This kind of reverb emulates the sound of small rooms with reflective surfaces and are great for adding a sense of depth and space to recordings. They have a quick decay time and are often used on vocals, strings, and brass instruments.

When choosing a reverb for a particular track, think about the style of music, the instrumentation, and the desired effect. Experiment with different types of reverbs and find the one that works best for your mix. Remember, the goal is to create a natural and spacious sound that complements the performance, not to overwhelm it with too much reverb.

Saturation

Saturation is a technique that involves adding harmonic distortion to a track, which results in a richer and fuller sound. The process simulates the subtle distortion characteristics of analog equipment, which can add warmth and character to a mix, making it sound more natural and vintage.

Saturation can be used to enhance individual tracks or to add cohesiveness to an entire mix. When used on individual tracks, it can add depth and warmth to vocals, guitars, drums, or any other instrument in the mix. When applied to the entire mix, it can help glue all the elements together, adding a cohesive and harmonious feel to the mix.

Plugins or hardware devices can be used to create saturation. Saturation plugins are a popular and affordable option that can be used directly within a DAW. There are several types of saturation plugins available, including tube emulators, tape saturation plugins, and harmonic exciters. These plugins allow you to control the amount of saturation applied to the track, the type of harmonic distortion, and the frequency range of the distortion.

When using saturation, exercise restraint and avoid overdoing it. Adding too much saturation can result in a muddy and unclear mix. Start with small amounts of saturation and gradually increase the effect until you achieve the desired result.

Using Automation and Creating Movement in a Mix

Automation can add dynamics and interest to a mix. It allows you to adjust the level, pan, and effects parameters of individual tracks over time, creating movement and shaping the sound of your mix.

Types of Automation

There are several types of automation that you can use to create movement in a mix:

- **Volume automation:** This type of automation adjusts the level of individual tracks over time. You can use volume automation to create dynamic changes in the mix, such as bringing up a guitar solo or bringing down the volume during a quiet section.
- **Pan automation:** This adjusts the placement of individual tracks in the stereo field over time. You can use this to create a sense of movement in the mix, such as panning a guitar from left to right during a solo.
- **Effect automation:** This automation adjusts the parameters of individual effects over time. You can use this to create interesting changes in the sound of a track, such as increasing the amount of reverb on a vocal during a chorus.
- **EQ automation:** This automation adjusts the frequency balance of individual tracks over time. You can use this to shape the tone of a track and create a more dynamic mix, such as boosting the low end of a bass during a breakdown.

Using Automation to Create Movement

Now that we've covered the different types of automation, let's take a look at how to use them to create movement in a mix.

One way to use automation is to create a sense of build and release. For example, you can gradually increase the volume and intensity of a track over time, building up to a climactic moment in the song. Then, you can release the tension by bringing the volume back down and removing some of the effects.

Automation can also be used as a tool to keep the listeners focus; this can be done by creating subtle variations in the mix. For example, you can use pan automation to move a guitar back and forth in the stereo field during a solo, or use EQ automation to make subtle changes to the tone of a vocal during a verse.

You can also use automation to create contrast between different sections of a song. For example, you can use volume automation to bring down the volume during a quiet section of a song, then bring it back up during the chorus to create a sense of tension and release.

Tips for Using Automation Effectively

Here are some tips for using automation effectively in your mixes

1. **Start with a plan:** Before you start automating, think about the overall arc of the song and how you want to use automation to create movement and interest.
2. **Use automation sparingly:** Too much automation can be distracting and take away from the overall sound of the mix. Only automate when it is necessary to get the

desired result.

3. **Be subtle:** Small changes can have a big impact on the sound of a mix. Don't be afraid to make subtle adjustments to the level, pan, or effects parameters of individual tracks.
4. **Use automation to solve problems:** If you're having trouble getting a particular track to sit well in the mix, try using automation to adjust its level, pan, or EQ.
5. **Don't forget about automation during mastering**: You can use automation to make small adjustments to the overall level and EQ of a mix during mastering. This helps to bring out the best in your mix.

Tips for Mixing Vocals, Drums, and Other Instruments

Let's take a look at some useful tips you can use when applying the techniques we have spoken about.

Tips for Mixing Vocals

1. **Start with a clean recording:** Before you start mixing vocals, make sure the recording is clean and free from any unwanted background noise, clicks, pops or distortions.
2. **Use your EQ to remove any unwanted frequency:** Every voice has a unique sound. To make it stand out in a mix, you need to remove unwanted frequencies. Any low-end rumble or high-end hiss that might be posing issues can be eliminated with EQ.
3. **Use compression to even out levels:** Vocals can have a wide dynamic range, which can make it difficult to balance them in a mix. Use compression to even out the levels and make them sit better in the mix.

4. **Use reverb and delay:** These can add depth and space to vocals and make them sit better in a mix. Use these effects sparingly to avoid making the vocals sound too wet or distant.
5. **Use automation to emphasize key phrases:** Automation is great for bringing key phrases to the forefront of the mix. Use volume automation to bring up the volume of important phrases or use EQ automation to highlight specific frequencies.

Tips for Mixing Drums

1. **EQ can be used as a tool to shape sound**: Every drum has a unique sound. To make them stand out in a mix, you need to shape their frequency response. Use EQ to remove unwanted frequencies and boost the frequencies that bring out the character of the drums.
2. **Use compression to even out levels:** Drums can have a wide dynamic range, which can make it difficult to balance them in a mix. Use compression to even out the levels and make them sit better in the mix.
3. **Use panning to create space:** A mix's feeling of width and space can be enhanced by panning. To create a harmonious and engaging mix, experiment with panning the drums to various locations in the stereo field.
4. **Depth and impact can be added with parallel processing:** This is especially useful for improving drums without making them sound too loud or overwhelming. Use parallel compression or parallel EQ to create a more interesting and impactful drum sound.
5. **Use automation to create movement:** This creates interest in a drum mix. Use volume automation to emphasize certain beats or use panning automation to

create a sense of movement in the stereo field.

Tips for Mixing Other Instruments

1. **Use EQ to shape the sound:** Every instrument has a unique sound. To make instruments stand out in a mix, you need to shape their frequency response. Use EQ to remove unwanted frequencies and boost the frequencies that bring
2. **Use compression to even out levels:** Other instruments can have a wide dynamic range, which can make it difficult to balance them in a mix. Use compression to even out the levels and make them sit better in the mix.
3. **Use panning to create space:** Experiment with panning the instruments to different positions in the stereo field to create a balanced and interesting mix.
4. **Use reverb and delay:** This can add depth and space to other instruments and make them sit better in a mix. Use these effects sparingly to avoid making the instruments sound too wet or distant.
5. **Use automation to create movement**: Volume automation emphasizes certain parts, while panning automation creates a sense of movement in the stereo field.

That's it for this chapter. In the next chapter we will take a look at the process of mastering…and how to master it.

CHAPTER 7
MASTERING

The final step during music production is mastering; that is, until the distribution and business side is addressed. In the process of mastering, a mix is polished and prepared for distribution to its intended audience. This involves enhancing the overall sound quality, tonal balance, dynamic range, and loudness of the song, as well as ensuring that it translates well across different playback systems. Mastering requires a combination of technical knowledge, critical listening skills, and artistic intuition to bring out the best in a mix while maintaining the integrity of the original vision. In this chapter, we will explore the fundamentals` of mastering and provide tips and techniques to help you achieve a professional-sounding master for your music.

Understanding the Role of Mastering in the Music Production Process

Mastering is the last step in the music production process. It's the process of taking a final mix and making sure that it sounds good on all types of playback systems, from headphones to club sound systems. Mastering is an art form that requires both technical expertise and a keen ear for detail.

At its core, mastering aims to enhance the sonic

characteristics of a track while maintaining its original artistic intent. The mastering engineer focuses on improving the clarity, depth, and overall impact of the music while also ensuring that it meets technical standards for distribution. This includes ensuring that the track has the right loudness, dynamic range, and tonal balance for different platforms.

With the advent of both louder speakers and bigger events it has now become more important than ever to be able to achieve a loud and competitive volume level without sacrificing the dynamic range and tonal balance of the music. Compression, limiting, and other tools that manage the music's dynamic range are used to do this.

Good tonal balance is a requirement for mastering a track. This involves ensuring that the different frequency ranges of the mix are well-balanced and that no single frequency is overpowering. This is mostly done with equalization to adjust the frequency response of the mix.

Mastering also involves creative processing to enhance the overall sound of the mix. This may include adding stereo width, harmonic excitement, or saturation to the mix to make it sound more vibrant and exciting. You'll also need to make sure that the transitions between tracks are smooth and that the overall sequence of songs flows well, if creating a mix or album.

You should keep in mind that mastering cannot fix a poorly recorded or mixed track. A good mix is the foundation of a great master, and so it's a good idea to invest time and effort into the mixing stage before sending the final mix for mastering.

Mastering Techniques for Achieving a Cohesive and Polished Sound

To ensure that the mix sounds consistent and clear across all speaker types and listening environments, mastering a song requires using a variety of tools like EQ, compression, limiting, and imagers. The ultimate aim of mastering is to create music that can compete with other professionally mastered tracks in the market, making it sound natural and appropriate when played on different platforms like radio, TV, streaming services, and other mediums. Though mastering music can be approached in different ways, we'll discuss some of the most commonly used steps to achieve a great sound.

The key steps involved in mastering a song include:

- **Finalizing the mix:** The first step in mastering is to ensure that your mix is complete and ready for the final mastering stage.
- **Bouncing down the stereo track:** When you're finished, bounce your mix down to a stereo track.
- **Beginning a new session:** Two things to carry out here are importing your stereo mix and making use of track referencing (Cortes, 2022).
- **Listening to the mix and taking notes:** While listening to the mix, make notes of areas that need improvement.
- **Adding clarity to the low end:** To increase the low end's clarity, use EQ.
- **Correcting the tone:** This can be done using EQ
- **Taming the dynamics and gluing the mix together:** Utilize compression to control the dynamics and bring the mix together.
- **Matching EQ adjustments to your reference:** To match

the balance of your reference songs, adjust the EQ.

- **Fixing or enhancing the stereo image:** This can be done using stereo imagers
- **Limiting the mix:** Use limiting to control the overall level of the mix.
- **Final mastering checks:** Listen to the final master and make any necessary adjustments.
- **Bouncing the master:** Once you're satisfied with the final master, bounce it down to a stereo file.

Finalizing the Mix

To prepare your mix for audio mastering, the first step is to ensure that it sounds balanced, cohesive, and has enough headroom for the mastering stage. Mastering should be considered a delicate art. Minor changes can significantly impact the overall mix, so you'll need to have a mix that sounds as close to the mastered version as possible.

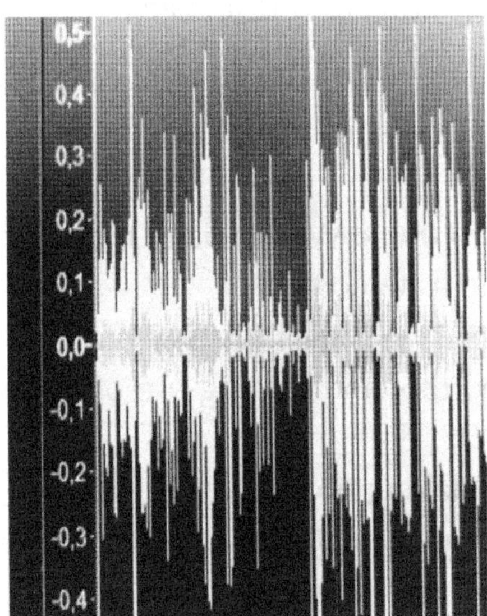

To improve a mix, it's a good idea to consider panning your instruments, as this creates a wider stereo image. You should also utilize proper mix bus processing techniques to improve the cohesiveness of the mix. Avoid clipping as much as possible because this will inject distortion into the mix that could be increased during mastering. Your mix should have a peak level between -3 and -6 dBFS and an average level of about -16 dBFS RMS.

Before bouncing down to a stereo file, make sure that you're satisfied with the level relationships between different elements of the mix. Once you have a stereo file or stems (if you prefer stem mastering), it's challenging to adjust levels without going back to the mixing stage of the audio production workflow.

Bouncing Down the Stereo Track

After completing your mix, you will have to export your session as an audio file. When bouncing your track down, you should use the same settings that you recorded with to ensure consistency. For instance, if you recorded in 24-bit resolution, make sure to bounce your file at 24-bit. Similarly, if you recorded at 48 kHz, ensure that you export your file at 48 kHz.

You must export your file in a lossless format like AIFF or WAV to retain the resolution of the original recording. Avoid exporting your file in MP3 format, as it will result in a loss of resolution.

Starting a New Session and Importing the Stereo Mix and Reference Tracks

Now that you have exported your audio, open a new project session and import your mix and reference tracks. Professionally made songs that represent how you want your own track to sound are referred to as reference tracks. Musicians often have specific songs, albums, or artists they aspire to emulate in their music. By using reference tracks, audio engineers can compare and contrast their mix or master to similar songs in the same genre or style. This process is an efficient way to track progress and ensure consistent results.

Using reference tracks can provide valuable insights into

how different elements of a song should sound, such as the low-end, vocals, or overall tonal balance. By comparing your mix to a reference track, you can identify areas that may require further attention and adjust your mix accordingly.

Listening to the Mix and Taking Notes

If you're new to mastering music, you might be wondering how to approach a mastering signal chain. The truth is, there isn't a one-size-fits-all solution for every track, as each mix has its own unique needs.

Before you apply any processing, take the time to listen to your track on different playback systems and take note of anything that stands out. Play the track on laptop speakers, headphones, in your car or anywhere else that you might have access to. Doing this will let you hear if your audio sounds good in a variety of circumstances or if there are any areas you need to adjust.

Apply all corrections before you add enhancements. Correcting spectral and dynamic problems first will allow you to prevent amplification of issues when applying a limiter, as a limiter raises the level of the quietest parts of your signal.

As you continue reading, keep in mind that the following steps in this chapter are processing solutions that can be applied if the mix requires it. Use your ears and trust your instincts when making decisions about what processing is necessary.

Adding Clarity to the Low End

Mastering the low end of a mix can be difficult, as the bass frequencies encompass various sounds, including the body of an acoustic guitar, the growl of saxophones, the weight of the bass guitar, and the punch of a kick drum. When several instruments occupy this range, the low end can become muddy and unfocused, compromising the overall sound quality.

To achieve clarity in the low end, consider using a Mid/Side EQ to add a high-pass filter to the Side channels. Bass frequencies that could otherwise bleed into the left and right channels will be reduced as a result. By making the low end more mono and narrowing its dynamic range, this technique prevents the low end from conflicting with other parts that are panned to the sides.

Correcting the Tone With EQ

When correcting the tone with EQ, you should approach it in a methodical and precise way. Start by listening to your mix and identifying frequency ranges that sound too loud or too quiet. You can use a spectrum analyzer to visually identify frequency imbalances in your mix.

Once you have identified the frequency ranges that need adjustment, use your EQ to make precise cuts or boosts to those frequencies. Be careful not to overdo it, as excessive EQ adjustments can introduce unwanted artifacts and distortions into your mix.

Always make EQ tweaks in the context of the entire mix. You may need to adjust the EQ settings of individual tracks to achieve the desired tonal balance in the overall mix. EQ adjustments made during mastering should be subtle and focused. The goal is to enhance the overall tonal balance of the mix, not to drastically alter its character.

When it comes to the order of EQ and compression in your mastering chain, the answer is not always clear-cut. A general rule of thumb is to start with corrective EQ before adding enhancements. If you hear frequencies that are problematic or distracting, use subtractive EQ to remove them. This will ensure that any subsequent processing, such as compression or saturation, doesn't amplify these issues.

Boosts or cuts of no more than 3 dB are recommended so as not to alter the overall balance of the mix. You can also adjust the Left/Right EQ, which lets you process the left and right channels independently. This is helpful when you want to address issues that are specific to one channel, such as a scraping sound on a guitar that's panned hard left.

Mid/Side EQ is another processing mode that separates the center from the sides of the stereo image. The sides only include information that is present in the left and right channels, but the middle, or "mid," contains mono information. To control the prominence of parts in the middle of the mix, mid/side EQ is frequently used. You can advance or recede particular components in the mix by using EQ on the midrange. The low-end can be trimmed down with a high-pass filter on the side channels, which will make it clearer and less muddy.

Taming the Dynamics and Gluing the Mix Together

A compressor is a powerful tool to help you achieve a well-balanced mix; there are two primary reasons for you to utilize a compressor. These reasons are adding glue and adding punch.

Adding glue refers to creating a cohesive and consistent mix with no distracting elements. A compressor can help even out the levels of different elements in the mix, creating a more balanced and enjoyable listening experience. Adding punch, is all about enhancing the transients in your mix, creating a more impactful and dynamic sound.

One way to achieve both glue and punch is through serial compression, which involves using multiple compressors in succession. Each compressor can be used for a specific purpose, with the first compressor attenuating the transients and the second compressor controlling the overall impact and punch.

Use compression subtly, with a maximum total gain reduction of no more than -3 dB. This is because compression applied to the entire mix can quickly become noticeable with even small adjustments.

While compression is a great tool for controlling the overall level of your mix, sometimes you need to be more surgical in your approach. This is where dynamic processing tools like multi-band compression, dynamic EQ, and spectral shaping come in handy. While dynamic EQ is better suited for the surgical removal of particular frequencies like resonances or unpleasant sibilance, multi-band compression is suitable for managing large frequency ranges. A low-ratio compression technique called spectral shaping provides a more clear and exact method of dynamic control.

Ultimately, it's up to you to decide which tools to use, but keep in mind that sometimes, all you need is a compressor (or two) to control the dynamics and add glue and punch to your track.

Making EQ Moves to Match Your Reference

Incorporating reference tracks into your mastering process can greatly benefit the final outcome of your music. By analyzing key elements such as frequency response and dynamic range, you can make informed decisions to align the overall aesthetic of your track with your desired sound. Utilizing reference tracks can prevent the loss of perspective during the mastering process. After prolonged listening, it's common for your ears to become fatigued and miss unwanted frequencies, such as high frequency build-up. Referencing your track against another can quickly highlight these discrepancies and provide a much-needed reset. Focus on making EQ adjustments that match the spectral profile of your chosen reference track.

Fixing or Enhancing the Stereo Image

After applying compression and EQ, you'll need to assess whether stereo widening or narrowing is necessary for your track. Adding stereo width can enhance the immersive experience of your mix, but be cautious as it can introduce phase issues that may degrade the quality of your mix when played in mono. You may want to narrow certain elements of the mix to improve clarity, such as bass frequencies that are present in the stereo image.

However, narrowing an element to mono can lead to a loss of information that exists in the left and right channels. Use stereo imaging plugins sparingly and just as necessary as a result. When selecting a stereo imager use one with a correlation meter that indicates your stereo file's mono compatibility.

Limiting the Mix

The final and arguably most important step in mastering a song is limiting. By using a limiter, you may raise your song's volume overall to match commercial loudness while keeping the peaks from going above 0 dBfs, the clipping point. A limiter is essentially a compressor with an extreme, brick wall ratio (:1) that, as the volume is increased, silences any sound that rises above the predetermined threshold.

Set your output/ceiling level to anywhere between -0.3 dB and -0.8 dB to start. It's important to maintain this level throughout the mastering process since it establishes the brick wall threshold right below the clipping point.

Next, you can turn up the gain until you achieve around -2 to -3 dB of gain reduction. However, it's important to exercise caution while increasing the gain because doing so beyond this point with a stock limiter can result in noise and undesired distortions.

Final Mastering Checks

You're almost finished. The final step is to ensure that your master has the appropriate dynamic range and loudness levels for your genre and delivery medium. Below is an in-depth look at the important qualities:

- **Loudness targets by genre:** When mastering a song, it is generally recommended to aim for an integrated loudness of at least -14 LUFS and a True Peak of -0.2 dBFS. However, the ideal loudness levels can vary depending on the genre. Target RMS values between -6 dBFS and -12 dBFS for louder genres including pop, rock, and EDM. For softer genres like folk, acoustic, and classical, you can aim as low as -16 dBFS.
- **Dynamic range:** This is a reference to the decibel (dB) differential in volume between the loudest and quietest sections of a song. It is important to maintain at least 6dB of dynamic range in your master to ensure that it retains its impact and interest. Without enough dynamic range, your music can sound flat and monotonous. Each genre may have a different ideal dynamic range. A classical piano piece might sound better with as much dynamic range as feasible, whilst an EDM tune might benefit from a narrower dynamic range.
- **Delivery mediums**: Each platform has a certain set of loudness standards and constraints that you have to deal with. For instance, if your track is not loud enough, streaming platforms may apply their own limiter that can

negatively impact your sound. Mastering for streaming is different from mastering for vinyl or CD, so it's crucial to do your research and understand the requirements of your chosen medium.

Bouncing the Master

Congratulations! You're now ready to export your song and share it with the world. Choose the music you wish to export as a lossless file (AIFF or WAV), as well as an .mp3 file for easy online distribution.

After selecting the appropriate file format and resolution, apply dithering to your track. When converting to lower bitrates, dithering adds a low-level noise to your audio to avoid distortion and other undesirable artifacts. You should only dither your audio once, as multiple dithering passes can actually degrade the quality of your track.

Now that you understand the music production process—from recording to mastering—it's time to take a look at some creative techniques for producing innovative music and collaborating with artists and musicians. Later on, we will discuss the business side of music production, from marketing to distribution, and even ethics. See you in the next chapter!

CHAPTER 8
MORE MUSIC PRODUCTION TECHNIQUES

In this chapter, we'll explore some exciting and innovative music production techniques, as well as offer tips on how to effectively collaborate with artists and musicians.

Creative Techniques for Producing Innovative Music

While there are many tried and true techniques that can produce great results, the most exciting music often comes from experimentation and pushing the boundaries of what's possible. So now, let's explore some creative techniques for producing innovative music. These techniques won't necessarily suit everyone's music style, but you'd be surprised by the difference they can make.

Unconventional Recording Methods

Experimenting with unconventional recording methods is an excellent way to add a unique touch to your music. By trying out different recording techniques, you can discover sounds and textures that you may not have thought possible with traditional methods. Examples of these methods are the following:

- **Recording with vintage equipment:** Consider using analog gear, such as vintage microphones, preamps, and tape machines, to achieve a vintage sound. This technique can work particularly well for genres such as blues, jazz, or classic rock.

- **Using found objects as instruments**: You could use everyday objects such as water bottles, cans, or even kitchen utensils as instruments. This technique works particularly well for genres such as experimental music, avant-garde, and sound art.
- **Recording outside in a natural environment:** You could record the sounds of birds, waves, or even traffic to create a unique soundscape. This technique works particularly well for genres such as ambient music, field recording, and soundscapes.
- **Using unusual microphone techniques:** By experimenting with microphone placement and techniques, you can create unique and unexpected sounds. For example, you could try using a contact microphone to capture vibrations from objects, or placing a microphone inside an acoustic guitar to capture the sound of the instrument's body.

Experimenting With Sound Design

Sound design is the art of creating and manipulating sounds to fit the desired mood and aesthetic of a piece of music. You may make completely original sounds by playing with sound design. Some of the methods you can use to do this include:

- **Modular synthesis:** Modular synthesizers are a powerful tool for sound design, allowing producers to create complex and evolving sounds by patching together various modules. This can be a highly experimental and exploratory process, as the producer can tweak and adjust the parameters of each module to achieve a desired sound. This technique is mostly good for genres such as experimental music, ambient, and techno.

- **Sampling:** This involves taking sounds from the real world and manipulating them in creative ways to create new and unique sounds. For example, a producer could record the sound of a door closing, and then manipulate it using effects such as delay, reverb, or distortion to create a textured sound. Hip-hop, electronic, and experimental music are among the genres where this method works especially well.
- **Granular synthesis:** This is a technique involving small sound fragments (or grains) that are manipulated and combined to create new textures and sounds. This can be done using software plugins, which allow the producer to manipulate the length, pitch, and amplitude of each grain. This technique is used for genres such as ambient, drone, and experimental music.
- **Foley and field recording:** Foley is the art of creating sound effects using everyday objects, while field recording involves capturing sounds from the real world. By recording and manipulating these sounds, producers can create unique textures and atmospheres that add depth and interest to their tracks. This technique is used for genres such as film and game music, as well as experimental music.
- **Instrument design:** By designing and building their own instruments, producers can create unique sounds that are specific to their music. This can involve using unusual

materials or combining different instruments to create hybrids. This technique is used in genres such as experimental music, noise, and avant-garde.

Incorporating Live Instruments

Electronic music production often relies heavily on software and digital instruments, but incorporating live instruments can add a human touch to your music. You could collaborate with musicians to record live instruments, or even learn to play an instrument yourself. By incorporating live instruments, you can add a level of depth and emotion to your music that can't be achieved with digital instruments alone.

Using Field Recordings

Field recordings are recordings of everyday sounds, such as the sounds of nature, cityscapes, or people's conversations. You can give your music a sense of place and ambience that can take the listener to a different place by adding these recordings into it. Another option is to experiment with editing field recordings to produce original soundscape.

Collaborating With Artists and Musicians

Collaboration is an important part of the music industry, and working with other artists and musicians can be an excellent way to expand your creative horizons and produce innovative music. However, collaboration can also be challenging, particularly when working with artists who have different musical backgrounds, tastes, and working styles.

There are some considerations you should make when working with other artists.

Be Clear With Your Roles and Expectations

Before beginning any collaboration, it's essential to establish clear roles and expectations for everyone involved. This includes discussing what each person's responsibilities will be, the timeline for the project, and any other important details. As a music producer, you may take on a variety of roles in a collaboration, such as overseeing the production process, providing guidance and feedback, and handling logistics such as scheduling and budgeting. Make sure that everyone involved is on the same page regarding their roles and responsibilities to avoid any confusion or misunderstandings later on.

Communicate Effectively

Clear communication is essential for any successful collaboration. Be sure to maintain regular communication with your collaborators throughout the process, and be open to feedback and suggestions. It's also important to communicate any change to the project (such as delays or shifts in the direction of the music) as soon as possible to avoid any surprises.

Respect Each Other's Creative Vision

When collaborating with artists and musicians, remember to

respect each other's creative vision and artistic direction. As a music producer, you should aim to provide guidance and support while allowing the artist to maintain their unique artistic vision. Avoid imposing your ideas on the artist or musician and instead work together to find a shared creative vision.

Embrace Different Perspectives

Collaborating with artists and musicians from different backgrounds and musical styles can lead to exciting and innovative music. Embrace the different perspectives and ideas that each collaborator brings to the project, and be open to trying new things. Remember that collaboration is an opportunity to learn and grow as a music producer and musician.

Establish a Positive Working Environment

Creating a positive working environment is key to a successful collaboration. This includes creating a welcoming and supportive space for all collaborators, establishing clear guidelines for behavior and communication, and maintaining a positive attitude throughout the process. By creating a positive working environment, you can foster creativity and collaboration and produce music that everyone involved is proud of.

In the next chapter, we will take a look at how music producers specialize in different industries.

CHAPTER 9
SPECIALIZATIONS IN MUSIC PRODUCTION

As music production has become increasingly popular and more accessible over the years, several specialized fields have emerged to highlight specific aspects of music creation and recording. In this chapter, we will explore some of these different fields and their main differences.

Film and TV Scoring

Film and TV scoring is a specialized field in music production that involves creating music to accompany visual media. It is an exciting and challenging area of music production that requires a unique set of skills and a deep understanding of storytelling through music. A scene in a movie or television show can frequently be made or broken by the music, which can also very quickly make the music producer involved famous!

Let's explore the world of film and TV scoring, and provide some tips for music producers who are interested in pursuing this career path.

Developing the Skills Needed for Film and TV Scoring

To become a successful film and TV composer, you need to develop several skills that are unique to this field. These skills include:

- **Strong composition skills:** You need to be able to create music that evokes emotion and tells a story. You'll need to be well-versed in both compositional methods and music theory.
- **Ability to work with video:** You need to be able to sync your music to the visual media. This requires an understanding of video editing software and the ability to work with timecode.
- **Collaboration skills:** Film and TV scoring is a collaborative process, and you need to be able to work closely with the director and other members of the production team.
- **Flexibility:** You need to be able to work within tight deadlines and to adapt your music to fit the changing needs of the production.

Tips for Music Producers Interested in Film and TV Scoring

If you are a music producer interested in film and TV scoring, here are some tips to help you get started:

- **Learn about the industry:** Read industry publications, attend industry events, and network with professionals in the field.
- **Develop a portfolio:** Create a portfolio of your best work, and make sure it showcases your ability to compose music that tells a story.
- **Familiarize yourself with video editing software**: Learn how to work with timecodes and sync your music to visual media.
- **Study the work of other composers:** Listen to the soundtracks of films and TV shows, and study the

composition techniques used by other composers.

- **Be prepared to start small**: Starting out in film and TV scoring often involves working on low-budget projects or short films.

Video Game Sound Design

Let's explore the world of video game sound design and provide some tips for music producers who are interested in pursuing this career path.

Developing the Skills Needed for Video Game Sound Design

To become a successful video game sound designer, you need to develop several skills that are unique to this field. These skills include:

- **Understanding of game audio middleware:** Learn how to use audio middleware systems such as Wwise, Fmod and Unity's audio engine.
- **Understanding of game audio implementation:** Understand how audio is integrated into video games through various techniques including layering, event-driven audio, and real-time processing.
- **Collaboration skills:** You need to be able to work closely with the game developer, programmers, and other members of the production team.
- **Sound design skills:** You need to be able to create unique sounds that enhance the gameplay experience, and make the game more immersive. This requires an understanding of sound design techniques and tools.
- **Flexibility:** You need to be able to work within tight deadlines and to adapt your audio to fit the changing needs of the game.

Tips for Music Producers Interested in Video Game Sound Design

Here are some pointers to get you started if you're interested in the sound design for video games.:

- **Learn about the industry**: Read industry publications, attend industry events, and network with professionals in the field.
- **Develop a portfolio:** Create a portfolio of your best work, and make sure it showcases your ability to create unique sounds that enhance the gameplay experience.
- **Familiarize yourself with game audio middleware and audio implementations:** Learn how to use and implement audio using middleware and techniques such as layering, event-driven audio and real-time processing.
- **Study the work of other sound designers:** Listen to the soundscapes of popular video games, and study the sound design techniques used by other sound designers.
- **Be prepared to start small:** When you start out in video game sound design, you will likely work on low-budget projects or small indie games.

Podcast and Radio Production

Podcasts and radio shows are popular platforms for sharing ideas, stories, and music with audiences. As a music producer, you can leverage your skills to create engaging and high-quality content for these platforms. Most radio hosts won't be producing music, at least not full time, but will still be required to create mixes that keep the audience entertained.

Developing the Skills Needed for Podcast and Radio Production

To become a successful podcast or radio producer, you need to develop several skills that are unique to this field. These skills include:

- **Audio editing:** You need to be proficient in audio editing software such as Audacity or Adobe Audition, which are used to edit and mix audio tracks.
- **Music production**: You must have a thorough knowledge of music theory, composing, and arrangement to be a successful music producer.
- **Sound design:** You should be familiar with sound design techniques and tools such as EQ, compression, and reverb.
- **Collaboration skills:** You should be comfortable working with the podcast or radio show host, and other members of the production team.
- **Time management:** You should be able to properly manage your time and complete tasks under pressure.

Tips for Music Producers Interested in Podcast and Radio Production

If you are a music producer interested in podcast and radio production, here are some tips to help you get started:

- **Listen to podcasts and radio shows:** Listen to a variety of podcasts and radio shows to get a sense of different styles, formats, and approaches.
- **Build your network:** Attend industry events, join online

forums and groups, and connect with other podcast and radio producers to build your network.

- **Create a demo reel**: This showcases your audio production skills, and you can use it to pitch to potential clients.
- **Be open to feedback:** Be open to feedback from clients and other members of the production team, and use it to improve your work.
- **Learn about copyright laws:** Understand copyright laws and licensing requirements for using music in your podcast or radio show.

Live Event Production

For music producers, live event production is a demanding and fascinating industry. Whether you're producing a concert, festival, or DJ-ing in your local club, the job of a live event producer is to create a memorable and engaging experience for the audience.

Developing the Skills Needed for Live Event Production

To become a successful live event producer, you need to develop several skills that are unique to this field. These skills include:

- **Event planning:** You need to be proficient in event planning and management, including coordinating with vendors, managing budgets, and creating timelines.
- **Music production:** You need to have a solid understanding of music theory, composition, and arranging.
- **Audio engineering:** You should be familiar with audio engineering tools and techniques such as mixing,

mastering, and sound reinforcement.

- **Video production**: You should be familiar with video production techniques and tools such as live streaming, recording, and post-production, to create a cohesive and engaging visual experience for the audience.
- **Collaboration skills:** You should be comfortable working with event organizers, performers, and other members of the production team.

Tips for Music Producers Interested in Live Event Production

If you are a music producer interested in live event production, here are some tips to help you get started:

- **Gain experience:** Volunteer at local events to gain experience and build your network.
- **Build your network:** Attend industry events, join online forums and groups, and connect with other live event producers.
- **Create a portfolio:** Your portfolio that showcases your live event production skills.
- **Be flexible:** Be open to last-minute changes and
- **Stay up-to-date**: Keep up-to-date with the latest technology and trends to stay competitive in the industry.

That's it for this chapter. Keep in mind that these are only the main fields open for music producers, and you'll probably be able to find a niche that suits your interests regardless of what they are.

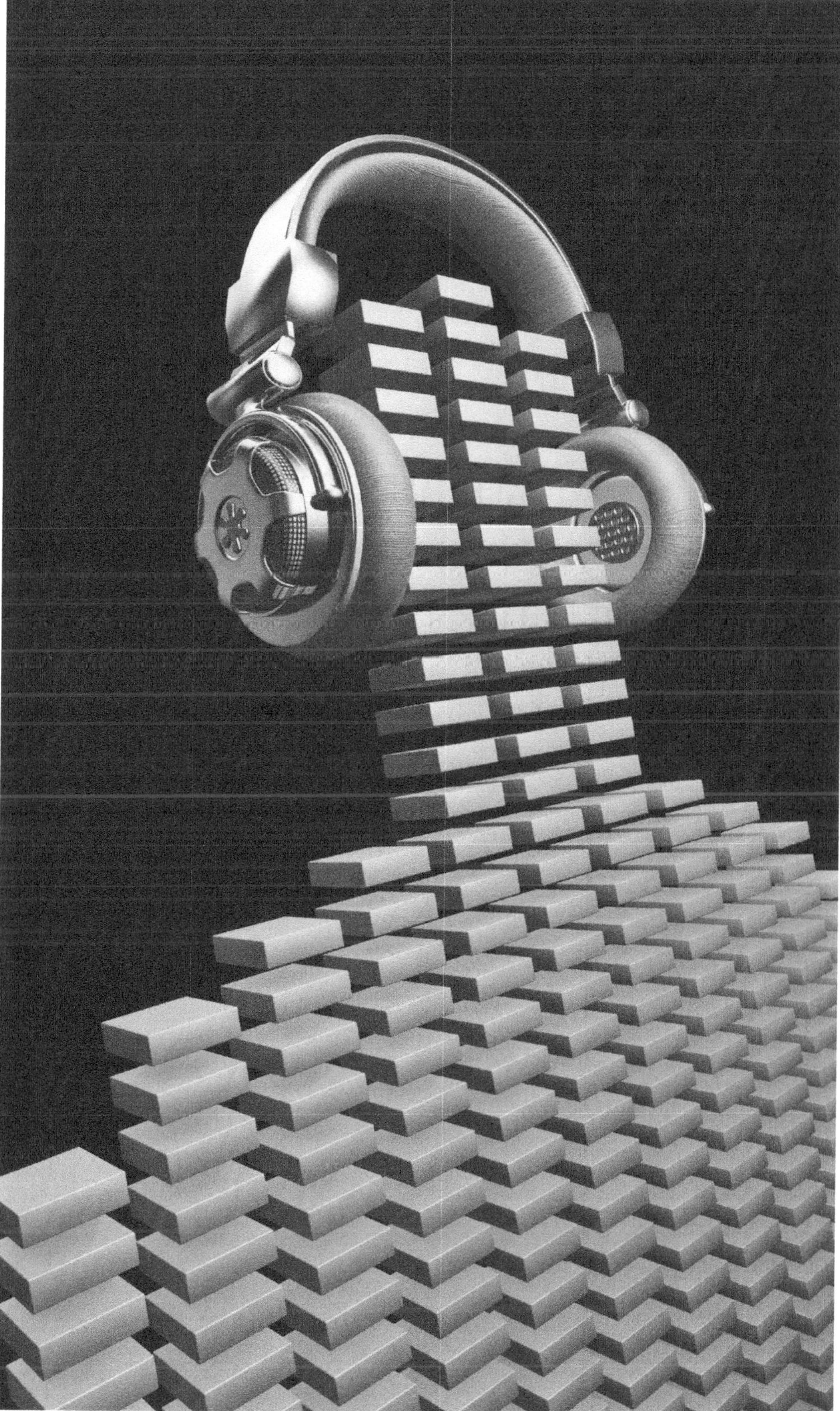

CHAPTER 10
ADVANCEMENTS IN MUSIC PRODUCTION TECHNOLOGY

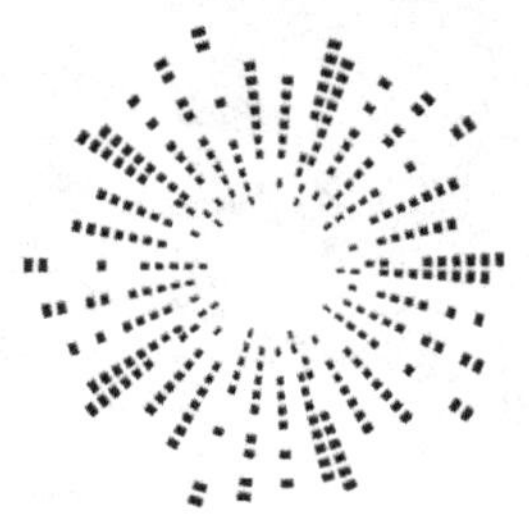

In recent years, there have been several significant advancements in music production technology. For instance, take the way that artificial intelligence (AI) has become an active ingredient in music composition. AI-powered software can analyze existing music and generate new compositions based on the analyzed patterns. This technology has been used in a variety of music genres, including classical, pop, and hip-hop. It should be noted, however, that the feasibility of these systems and their usefulness is debatable, at least for the moment.

The use of virtual reality (VR) and augmented reality (AR) to create immersive musical experiences is another fascinating advancement in music production technology. This technology allows users to feel like they are inside a music video or concert venue, making for a truly unique experience.

Cloud-based music production tools have also been developed, allowing musicians to collaborate on music projects remotely. Real-time cooperation is made possible by this technology, which is very helpful when working with artists that are spread out across different regions.

Modular synthesizers have been around for decades, but

recent advancements have made them more accessible and easier to use. These systems allow musicians to create custom synthesizer setups, which can produce unique sounds.

High-resolution audio technology has been developed to capture audio with greater accuracy and detail. This technology is particularly useful in professional music production, where sound quality is crucial.

DAWs are computer software programs that give artists the ability to record, edit, and mix music. Recent advancements in DAWs have made them more user-friendly, intuitive, and powerful.

Mobile music production technology has evolved rapidly in recent years. Musicians can now produce music on their smartphones or tablets using apps that offer powerful audio processing tools. This development has made music production more accessible, affordable, and intuitive than ever before. As technology continues to evolve, we can assume lot's more new developments in music production.

Digital Audio Workstations (DAWS)

These tools have become increasingly popular over the years, as technology has made it easier and more affordable for musicians to produce high-quality music from their own home studios.

DAWs come in various shapes and sizes, from basic freeware to complex professional-grade software. The most popular DAWs include Logic Pro, Ableton Live, Pro Tools, Cubase and FL Studio. Each of these software applications has its own strengths and weaknesses, but they all share common features that allow users to create and manipulate digital audio.

One of the primary functions of a DAW is to record audio. Musicians can use a DAW to record live instruments, vocals, or any other type of audio. The software allows users to adjust the recording settings, such as sample rate and bit depth, to ensure high-quality recordings.

After recording, users can edit the audio within the DAW. Individual tracks may be edited in terms of time, pitch, and volume, and effects like reverb, delay, and compression may also be added. Many DAWs also include virtual instruments, which allow users to create digital versions of acoustic instruments such as pianos, drums, and guitars.

Once the audio has been recorded and edited, users can mix the tracks together to create a final product. Mixing involves adjusting the levels of each track to establish a balanced and cohesive sound. It also involves adding EQ and other effects to enhance the overall sound quality.

DAWs are becoming a necessary tool for sound engineers, producers, and artists. They have allowed musicians to produce high-quality music from their own home studios, eliminating the need for expensive recording studios. They have also made it easier for musicians to collaborate remotely, as tracks can be easily shared and edited within the software.

While DAWs have revolutionized the music industry, they do require some technical expertise to use effectively. Learning how to use a DAW can take time and effort, but with practice, users can create professional-sounding music from their own home studios.

Using a DAW can be a bit intimidating for beginners, but with some guidance, it can be a powerful tool for music production. Let's explore how to use a DAW:

1. **Choose your DAW:** There are numerous DAWs available, each with its own set of functions and user interface. Choose the one that best fits your needs and budget.
2. **Set up your audio interface:** This piece of hardware links your computer to your audio equipment. Setup instructions from the manufacturer should be followed after connecting your audio interface to your computer.
3. **Create a new project:** Once your audio interface is set up, create a new project in your DAW. This is where you'll build your music from scratch.
4. **Track addition:** Include a new track in your project. The "Add Track" button or a keyboard shortcut can be used to accomplish this. Select the track type, such as an audio track or a MIDI track, that you want to add.
5. **Record audio:** Arm the track for recording and click the "Record" button to start recording audio. Record your audio, then stop the recording when you're finished. You can then edit your audio using various tools in your DAW.
6. **Add MIDI:** If you're working with MIDI, add a new MIDI track to your project. This will allow you to use virtual instruments or hardware synthesizers to create sounds.

You can then program MIDI notes using a piano roll editor or by playing a MIDI controller.

7. **Edit your music:** Once you've recorded audio or added MIDI, you can edit your music using various tools in your DAW. This can include editing the timing of MIDI notes, adding effects to audio tracks, or adjusting the volume and panning of individual tracks.
8. **Mix your music:** Once you've finished editing your music, you can mix it by adjusting the levels of individual tracks, applying effects like reverb and compression, and adding automation to create dynamic changes.
9. **Export your music**: Once you've finished mixing your music, export it as a stereo WAV or .mp3 file. This will allow you to share your music with others or upload it to streaming platforms.

Keep in mind that all DAWs will have slightly different interfaces and may be more or less easy to use. Most DAWs will have a user manual and/or tutorials to help you. Consider using a demo or trial version first to see which DAW works best for you and your hardware.

Some additional tips to keep in mind:

- Take advantage of keyboard shortcuts to speed up your workflow. Most DAWs have a list of keyboard shortcuts that you can reference.
- To create a professional sound, use reference tracks. Compare your mix to other music in the same genre and adjust accordingly.
- Experiment with different plugins and effects to find the sound you're looking for. Don't be afraid to try

something new.

- Practice regularly to develop your skills. The more you use your DAW, the more comfortable you'll become with it.

Virtual Instruments and Plugins

Virtual instruments and plugins are software-based tools that allow musicians and producers to create digital versions of acoustic instruments and effects. These tools have become an essential part of modern music production, allowing musicians to produce high-quality music from their own home studios.

Virtual instruments come in various shapes and sizes, from simple synthesizers to complex orchestral libraries. These software-based instruments can be used to create digital versions of any acoustic instrument, including pianos, drums, guitars, and strings. Virtual instruments can be played using a MIDI keyboard, which sends digital signals to the software to trigger the corresponding notes.

Plugins are software-based effects that can be used to enhance the sound of digital audio. Plugins can be used to add reverb, delay, compression, distortion, and many other effects to individual tracks or the overall mix. They can be inserted into a DAW and controlled using a graphical user interface.

Virtual instruments and plugins have many advantages over traditional acoustic instruments and effects. They are much more affordable than their physical counterparts, and they can be easily customized and manipulated to achieve a desired sound. Virtual instruments also allow musicians to access a vast library of sounds that may be difficult or impossible to replicate with traditional instruments.

One of the most significant advantages of virtual instruments and plugins is their ability to be updated and improved. Manufacturers can release updates and new versions of their software, allowing musicians to access new sounds and features. This makes virtual instruments and plugins a sound investment for musicians and producers, as they can continue to use the software for years to come.

Despite their advantages, virtual instruments and plugins do have some limitations. They may not be able to replicate the nuances and subtleties of acoustic instruments, particularly for experienced musicians. Virtual instruments can also require a significant amount of processing power, which can be a limitation for some users.

Virtual Studio Technology (VST)

VST stands for Virtual Studio Technology, and it's a software interface created by Steinberg that allows third-party software to be integrated with DAWs. VST plugins are essentially digital instruments or effects that can be used within a DAW to create and manipulate sounds. They can range from simple synthesizers and samplers to complex processors that simulate analog equipment, like compressors and equalizers.

How Do VST Plugins Work?

When a VST plugin is loaded into a DAW, it becomes a part of the software and can be accessed just like any other built-in feature. VST plugins can be used to manipulate individual tracks, apply effects to groups of tracks, or even add global effects to the entire mix. Most VST plugins are user-friendly, and once they're loaded into the DAW, they can be controlled with a series of knobs and sliders.

To use a VST plugin with a DAW, you'll need to follow a few basic steps:

1. **Begin by installing the plugin on your computer set:** Most VST plugins come with an installer that will guide you through the installation process. Make sure to follow the instructions carefully to ensure that the plugin is installed correctly.
2. **Open your DAW**: Once the VST plugin is installed, open your DAW. Most DAWs will automatically scan for new plugins when they're launched, so your VST plugin should appear in the list of available plugins.
3. **Load the VST plugin onto a track:** In your DAW, create a new track and select the VST plugin you want to use. This can usually be done by opening the plugin browser and selecting the plugin from the list. Drag & drop the plugin into the track after choosing it.
4. **Configure the VST plugin:** Once the plugin is loaded onto the track, you'll need to configure it to suit your needs. This can be done by adjusting the plugin's settings, which are typically accessible via a series of knobs, sliders, and buttons.
5. **Utilize the VST plugin to produce and edit sounds:** With the VST plugin configured, you can now use it to create and manipulate sounds in your DAW. For example, if you're using a synthesizer plugin, you can use it to create a melody or a bassline. If you're using an effects plugin, you can use it to add reverb, delay, or distortion to a track.
6. **Save your project:** Once you've finished working with the VST plugin, make sure to save your project to ensure that your progress is preserved.

Some additional tips to keep in mind:

- It's a good idea to familiarize yourself with the documentation for your VST plugin, as this will give you a better understanding of how to use it.
- Make sure to check for software updates for both your DAW and your VST plugins regularly, as this can help ensure that everything works smoothly.
- Be patient and take the time to experiment with different plugins and settings. With practice, you'll develop a better understanding of how to use VST plugins to achieve the sound you're looking for.

Virtual and Augmented Reality Production Techniques

Virtual and augmented reality (VR/AR) production techniques are increasingly b`eing used in music production to create immersive experiences for fans and artists. The technology has come a long way since its first iterations in the '90s and while it hasn't quite reached the level of sci-fi films and books from that period, it has had a big impact on the entertainment industry. These techniques allow musicians to create virtual concerts, music videos, and other interactive experiences that bring fans closer to the music:

- **Virtual concerts:** These are becoming more popular, especially in light of the COVID-19 pandemic, which has made it difficult for artists to tour and perform in person. Artists may now create virtual concerts that anybody in the world can watch thanks to VR technology. Fans can experience the concert in a fully immersive environment, feeling as though they are in the same room as the artist. These concerts can be created using a combination of 3D modeling, motion capture, and CGI techniques. The artist can perform in a green screen studio, which allows them to be placed in a virtual environment that can be viewed by fans wearing VR headsets. These concerts can also include interactive elements, such as crowd noise and the ability to interact with other fans.

- **Music videos:** This is another area where VR/AR production techniques are being used. VR music videos allow fans to experience the music in a fully immersive environment, with the artist or band placed in a virtual environment that matches the mood and tone of the music.
- **AR music videos:** These allow fans to interact with the music video in a more interactive way. Using their smartphone or tablet camera, fans can overlay digital content onto the real world, creating an augmented reality experience that blends the music video with the physical environment.
- **Interactive experiences:** VR/AR production techniques are also being used to create interactive experiences for fans. This can include virtual meet and greets, where fans can interact with the artist in a virtual environment; and immersive music experiences, where fans can explore a virtual environment inspired by the music. These experiences can be created using a combination of 3D modeling, motion capture, and interactive software. The artist can create a virtual avatar that can be used to interact with fans in a fully immersive environment.

As we move into the next chapter, we'll dive into the

fascinating world of music production's business side. Join me as we explore the various aspects of music production that drive success—from marketing strategies to revenue streams. See you there!

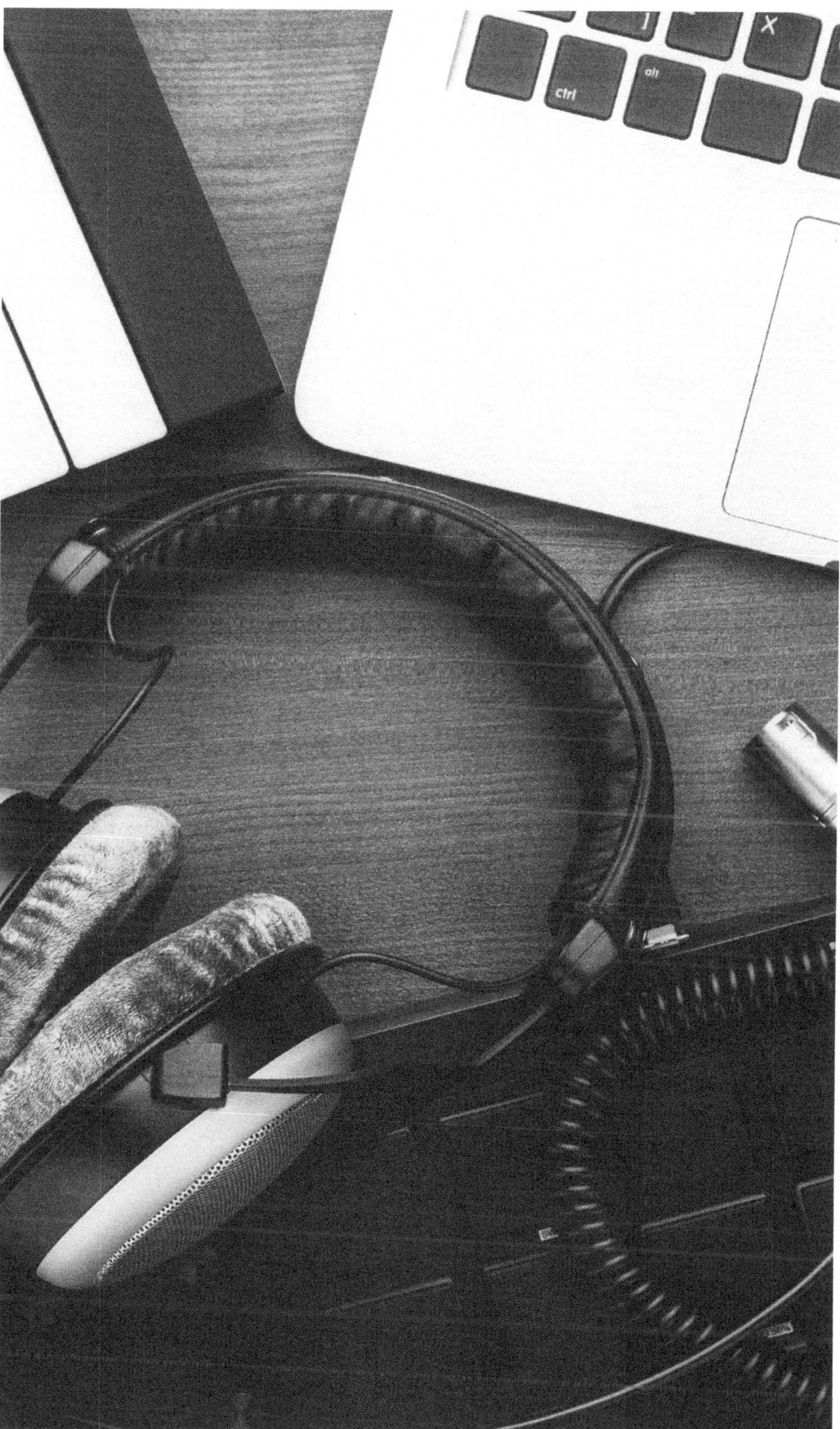
X
alt
ctrl

CHAPTER 11
BUSINESS IN MUSIC PRODUCTION

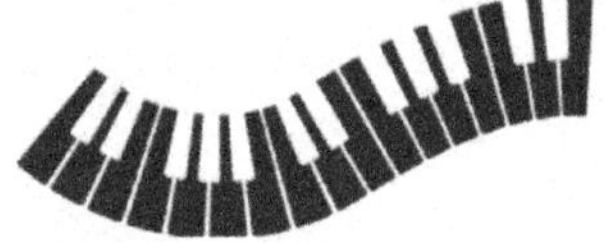

While music production is often associated with creativity and artistic expression, it is also a business. For music producers to be successful in the market, they must have a solid understanding of the business side of the production process. Without a solid understanding of the financial, legal, and marketing aspects of music production, it can be difficult to build a sustainable career as a music producer.

Knowing how to market and promote music effectively, secure profitable revenue streams, and navigate legal and financial considerations are all crucial elements of music production. By understanding these aspects of the music industry, music producers can make informed decisions, build strong partnerships and collaborations, and ultimately achieve greater success in their careers.

Marketing Strategies

Marketing is a crucial aspect of the music industry, and it is essential for music producers to have a solid understanding of marketing principles and techniques. Effective marketing can help music producers promote their work, build a following, and increase their visibility in the industry. By marketing their music effectively, music producers can reach new audiences, attract new fans, and generate revenue from their work.

A solid brand identity can be developed with the aid of marketing. By developing a consistent visual and sonic aesthetic and promoting that aesthetic across all marketing channels, music producers can establish a unique identity that sets them apart from other producers in the industry. This can help to build a loyal following of fans who identify with their brand and are more likely to support their work.

By using social media, email marketing, paid advertising, and other promotional tactics, music producers can build anticipation for their music releases and generate excitement among fans. This can help to increase the likelihood that fans will listen to their music, purchase their work, and attend their shows.

By using marketing tactics to build a following and generate revenue, music producers can demonstrate their value to the industry and attract the attention of industry professionals, such as managers, agents, and labels. For music producers, this may help to open doors and generate new prospects.

So, let's take a closer look at marketing and explore how you can implement it in your music production journey!

Different Marketing Methods

There are a variety of marketing methods that a music producer can use. Let's take a look at some of the most common and successful methods.

Social Media Marketing

Social media platforms such as Instagram, Twitter, Facebook, and TikTok are all useful tools for music producers to connect with fans, promote their work, and build a following. Social media marketing involves creating and sharing engaging content such as music clips, behind-the-scenes footage, and photos to build a strong online presence and foster a relationship with fans.

Posting content on social media regularly is critical to maintain engagement with your fans and create momentum for your work. However, you should focus on the quality of your content to make it visually appealing and showcase your music to the best of its potential. You can use high-quality images and videos, and ensure that your audio is mixed and mastered professionally.

Engage with your followers by responding to their comments and messages, creating a sense of community around your work, and increasing loyalty. Utilize pertinent hashtags to connect with a wider audience, and look for trending hashtags in your industry to use in your postings.

Collaborating with other artists is an excellent way to expand your reach on social media. By working with other artists, you can tap into their fan base and gain new followers. It's a terrific way to network in the music business, too.

Running promotions and contests can generate excitement around your music and engage your audience. Consider offering a giveaway or discount code for your merchandise in order to drive sales.

Email Marketing

Email marketing involves sending targeted promotional emails to fans and subscribers to promote new releases, upcoming shows, and merchandise sales. Music producers can use email marketing to stay in touch with their fans, build anticipation for new releases, and drive sales. Here are some guidelines for getting started with email marketing.

- **Build an email list:** Begin by obtaining the email addresses of your supporters and fans. You can do this by adding a sign-up form on your website or social media pages, or offering an incentive such as a free download or exclusive content in exchange for signing up.
- **Choose an email marketing service:** Such email marketing tools like Mailchimp, Constant Contact, and Campaign Monitor are readily available. Choose a service that fits your budget and has the features you need to create and send professional-looking emails.
- **Design your emails:** Your emails should be visually appealing and showcase your music. Include a call-to-action such as asking your subscribers to listen to your new release or follow you on social media. It's a good idea to optimize your emails for phones and tablets.
- **Segment your list:** This allows you to send targeted messages to specific groups of subscribers. For example, you can segment your list by location or music genre and send personalized emails based on their interests.
- **Set up automation:** This allows you to send emails automatically based on subscriber behavior or actions. For example, you can set up a welcome series for new subscribers or send a follow-up email to those who clicked on a link in your previous email.
- **Analyze your results:** Use the analytics provided by your email marketing service to track open rates, click-through

rates, and other metrics. You can use this to enhance your email efforts and gradually boost your results.

Paid Advertising

Paid advertising involves paying to promote music and events on platforms such as Google AdWords, Facebook Ads, and Instagram Ads. Paid ads are great for targeting specific people. It can be very useful for promoting new releases or upcoming shows.

Influencer Marketing

Influencer marketing is collaborating with bloggers or social media influencers to market music and events to their audiences. Music producers can work with influencers in their genre or with a similar fanbase to reach new audiences and build their brand.

Content Marketing

Content marketing involves creating valuable and informative content such as blog posts, podcasts, and videos to engage fans and build a following. Music producers can create content that speaks to their fans' interests and passions to build a strong relationship with their audience.

Livestreaming

Livestreaming involves broadcasting live shows or behind-the-scenes footage on platforms such as YouTube, Twitch, or Instagram Live. Livestreaming can help music producers connect with fans in real-time and create a sense of community around their work. With some sites like YouTube, it can even be a major source of income and encouragement.

Music producers have a range of marketing strategies at their disposal to promote their work, build a following, and generate revenue. By using a combination of these tactics, you can create a strong online presence, connect with fans, and grow your career in the music industry. Consider working with someone that has studied search engine optimization (SEO) or taking a course yourself. Looking up successful artists and emulating their marketing strategies can also help.

Revenue Streams

As a music producer, there are several revenue streams available that can help you make money from your music. These include, but are not limited to:

- **Royalties:** These are payments that music producers receive when their music is played on the radio, TV, streaming platforms, or in public places like bars and restaurants. Performing rights organizations (PROs) like ASCAP, BMI, and SESAC often collect these fees.
- **Sales:** Music producers can sell their music through various channels such as digital download platforms like iTunes and Bandcamp, physical sales such as CDs and vinyl records, and merchandise such as t-shirts and posters.
- **Streaming:** Music creators receive royalties from streaming services like Tidal, Apple Music, and Spotify for each song that is played. While the payouts may be small, streaming can generate a significant revenue stream if you have a large following.
- **Sync licensing:** This involves licensing your music for use in films, TV shows, commercials, video games, and other media. This can be a lucrative revenue stream, but it requires networking and building relationships with music supervisors and licensing agencies.

- **Performance income:** Music producers can earn income by performing live shows, DJ sets, and other live events. This revenue stream requires building a fanbase and booking gigs, but can be very profitable.
- **Production fees:** Music producers can charge production fees for their services in creating and producing music for other artists. This revenue stream can be significant if you are in high demand and can command a high fee.

Financial Management

Budgeting, accounting, and bookkeeping are some fundamental financial management concepts that can assist you in keeping track of your income and expenses, making wise financial decisions, and achieving your financial objectives.

Budgeting

Budgeting is an important part of managing your finances and ensuring the success of your business. Creating a budget entails making a strategy for your future income and expenses. This involves estimating your income, identifying your expenses, and allocating funds accordingly.

When creating a budget, you will want to start by estimating your income for the upcoming month or quarter. As a music producer, your income may come from various sources such as royalties, sales, streaming, and performance income.

Once you have estimated your income, you'll identify your expenses, though if you aren't able to estimate your income you can start with your expenses first, so that you at least have an idea of how much you'll need to make to cover everything. Your expenses may include studio rent, equipment, software, marketing, and any other business-related expenses. Be thorough when identifying your expenses and account for both fixed and variable expenses.

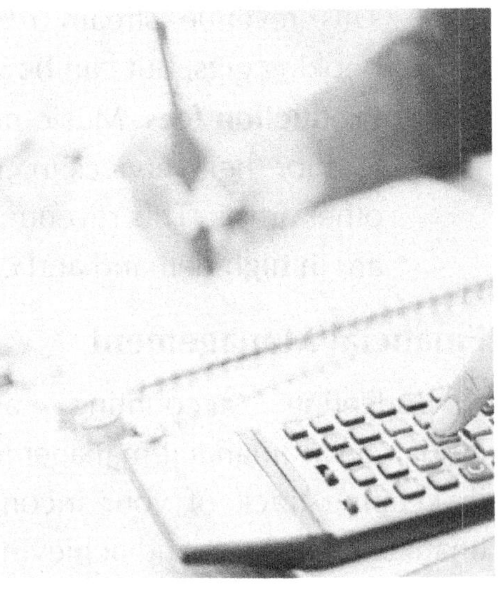

Rent and insurance are examples of fixed expenses that don't alter from month to month. Variable costs include things like marketing and equipment purchases that can change from month to month. By identifying your fixed and variable expenses, you can better understand where your money is going and make adjustments if you need to.

After identifying your income and expenses, you need to allocate your funds based on your priorities and goals. This involves deciding how much money to allocate to each expense category, and making sure that your expenses do not exceed your income.

For example, if you want to invest in new equipment or software, allocate more funds towards those expenses. If you want to focus on marketing, allocate more funds towards social media advertising or email marketing campaigns. By prioritizing your expenses, you can make sure that your money is being used in the most effective way possible.

Review your budget on a regular basis to ensure that you are staying on track. This involves monitoring your income and expenses, and making adjustments as needed. For example, if you are not generating as much income as you expected, you may need to cut back on expenses or find ways to increase your income. Conversely, if you are generating more income than expected, you may have more funds available to invest in your business.

There are a lot of both free and paid apps that you can use to help you budget. If you are using Microsoft Office for your business needs you can create a new document and download a template to use as a budget. Experiment with some different options and find what works best for you.

Accounting

Accounting entails logging, categorizing, and summarizing financial activities in order to shed light on your company's financial situation. It is essential for making informed financial decisions and ensuring compliance with tax laws and regulations.

To practice basic accounting, start by organizing your financial records. Separate company and personal costs, and keep track of all revenue and expenditures. To keep track of your finances and produce reports, its a good idea to use accounting software like QuickBooks or Xero.

Regularly review your financial reports to gain insight into your business's financial health. Look for trends, identify areas for improvement, and adjust your budget accordingly.

Bookkeeping

An essential component of managing your funds is bookkeeping. This involves recording and organizing financial transactions in an organized and systematic manner by keeping track of income and expenses, creating invoices, and reconciling bank statements.

You must accurately document all of your financial

transactions. Accounting software or simply a spreadsheet like Microsoft Excel or Google Docs can be used for this. Be detailed when recording your transactions, and include all relevant information such as the date, amount, description, and the account affected.

By maintaining reliable records, you can track the financial health of your company, pinpoint areas for improvement, and base choices on the financial information. Bookkeeping can also help you a great deal in your tax planning and preparation, by providing a clear and organized record of all financial transactions.

Invoices serve as a record of services provided or goods sold, and provide a means for clients to make payments. Include information on the items or services supplied, the date, and the amount when producing invoices. Invoicing software can help automate the process and ensure that all invoices are created and sent in a timely manner.

Payments that are received by you will also need to be tracked. This includes payments from clients, royalties or anything else that brings money into your business. This will help individuals keep track of outstanding payments and ensure that you get paid for your services.

Reconciling bank statements involves comparing financial records with bank statements to make sure that all transactions are recorded accurately. By reconciling bank statements regularly, you can identify discrepancies or errors and make corrections as needed. This will help keep your financial records up-to-date and ensure that an accurate picture of your financial situation is maintained.

Effective bookkeeping can help you in making important financial decisions, such as investments, hiring employees, or expanding the business. By having a clear and organized record of financial transactions, you make sure that you have enough cash to cover your expenses, and decide when and if you need to make any changes.

As you grow and start having more clients you may want to hire an accountant, many accountants will also handle the bookkeeping, or you might want to hire an in-house bookkeeper. They can also sometimes provide financial advice and make sure that your business is meeting its legal obligations to the tax man.

Going Independent vs. Using a Record Label

The choice of joining a record label or going independent is one that music producers frequently have to make. While there are benefits to both options, it ultimately depends on the goals and priorities of the producer. In this section, we'll discuss the pros and cons of going independent versus using a record label.

Going independent means that a music producer releases their music on their own, without the support of a record label. Here are some of the benefits of going independent:

- **Creative control:** When you go independent, you have complete control over your music. You can create whatever you want without having to worry about what a record label might want or expect from you.
- **Higher profits:** When you don't have a record label taking a percentage of your earnings, you get to keep more of the money you make. This can be especially beneficial for smaller producers who are just starting out and may not have a large fan base yet.
- **Flexibility:** Being independent means that you can release music whenever you want and however you want. You don't have to wait for approval from a record label or follow their release schedule.
- **Fan engagement:** Going independent can also allow for more direct engagement with fans. Without a record label acting as a middleman, you can build a closer relationship with your audience and build a more loyal following.

However, going independent also has its drawbacks:

- **Limited resources:** Without the support of a record label, you'll need to handle everything yourself, from recording and production to marketing and distribution. This can take a lot of work and a large time and financial commitment.
- **Lack of connections:** Record labels have connections in the music industry that can be difficult to establish on your own. This can make it harder to get your music heard by a larger audience or to secure high-profile gigs.
- **Limited exposure:** Without a record label to help promote your music, it can be challenging to get your music in front of new listeners. This can make it harder to build a fan base

and grow your career.

Using a Record Label

Using a record label means that you sign with a company that will handle the production, distribution, and marketing of your music. Here are some of the benefits of using a record label:

- **Resources:** A record label can provide you with the resources you need to make your music and build your career. They can handle the production, marketing, and distribution of your music, which can save you time and money.
- **Industry Networking:** Industry contacts can be challenging to develop on your own, but record labels have ties in the music business. This can help you secure high-profile gigs, get your music played on the radio, and collaborate with other artists.
- **Exposure:** Record companies can help you spread the word about your music, which can help you gain more fans and advance your career.

However, using a record label also has its drawbacks:

- **Loss of creative control**: When you sign with a record label, you may be required to follow their expectations and creative direction. This can limit your ability to create the music you want to make.
- **Profit sharing:** Record labels take a percentage of your earnings, which can significantly reduce your profits.
- **Contractual obligations**: When you sign with a record label, you'll likely be required to sign a contract that outlines your obligations and restrictions. This can limit your flexibility and creative freedom.

In the next chapter, we will explore the role of ethics in music production. See you there!

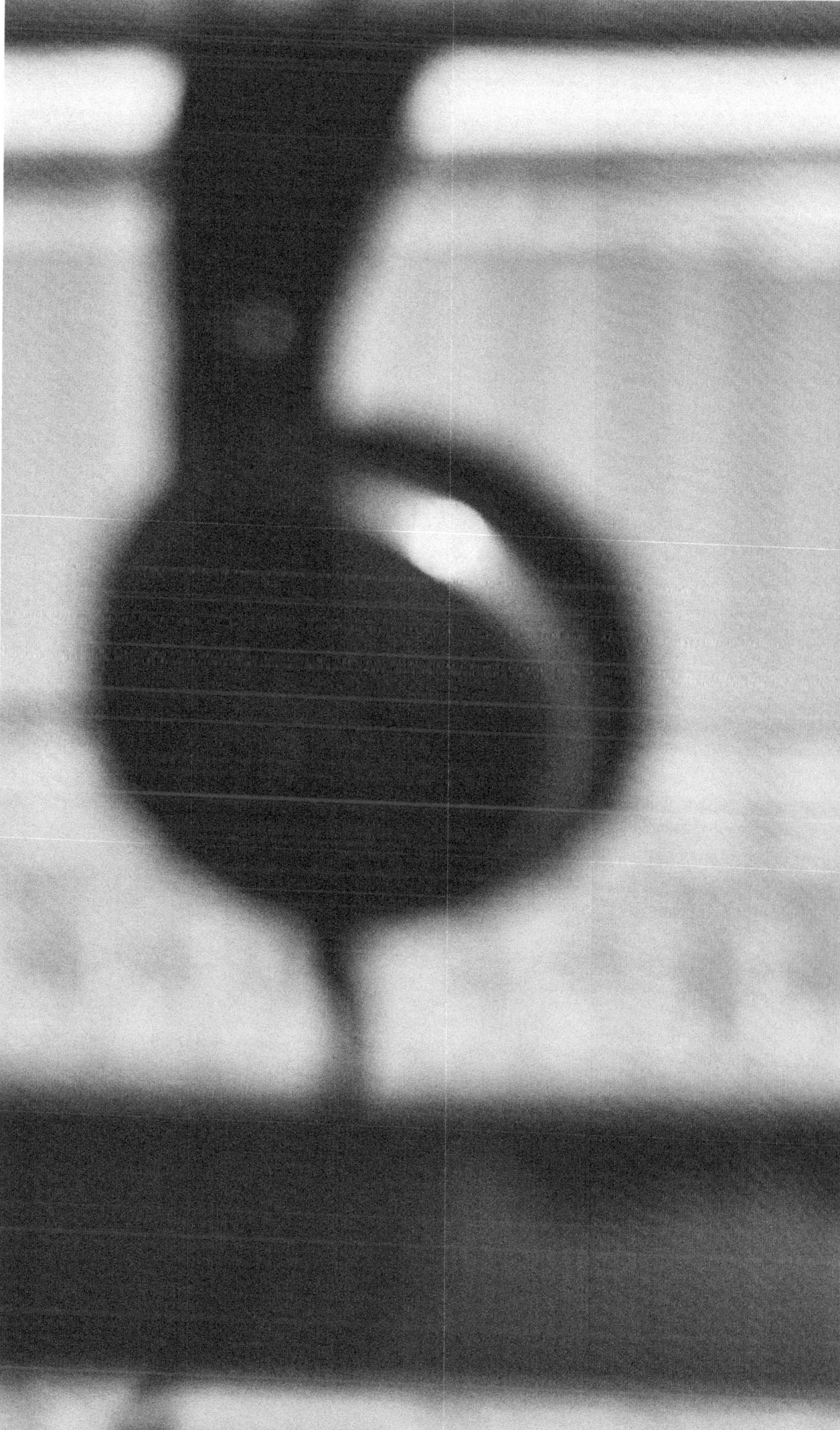

CHAPTER 11

ETHICS IN MUSIC PRODUCTION

Ethical considerations are an essential aspect of any industry, and that includes music production. As music producers, you need to be aware of ethical issues and considerations that may arise in the course of our work. This can include issues related to copyright, sampling, artist collaboration, and representation.

One of the primary ethical considerations in music production is copyright. It is essential to ensure that all music used in a production is properly licensed or cleared, and that all royalties and payments are made to the appropriate parties. This not only protects the rights of artists and songwriters, but also ensures that your own work is protected from legal action.

Sampling is a useful creative tool, but you must obtain permission or properly license any sample used in a production. Failure to do so can result in legal action and damage to your reputation.

Collaborations with artists would be another area where ethical considerations may come into play. Ensure that all artists are treated fairly and with respect, and that their rights and interests are protected. This can include issues such as fair compensation, credit, and creative control. It is also important to ensure that all artists and groups are represented accurately and respectfully, without perpetuating harmful stereotypes or cultural appropriation.

With that out of the way, let's take a closer look at some of the ethical considerations in the music industry.

The Importance of Fair Compensation and Rights for Artists and Musicians

One of the primary issues facing artists and musicians is the lack of fair compensation for their work. This can take many forms, such as low or non-existent royalties, unpaid performances, or exploitative contracts. Many artists and musicians struggle to make a living from their work, and may be forced to take on other jobs or sacrifice their creative pursuits in order to make ends meet.

This lack of fair compensation not only harms individual artists and musicians, but also has broader implications for the music industry as a whole. Without adequate compensation, it becomes increasingly difficult for artists and musicians to sustain their careers and continue creating new music. This can lead to a decline in the quality and diversity of music available, and ultimately harm the industry as a whole.

The protection of artists' and musicians' rights is also very important. This includes issues like copyright and intellectual property, but also extends to issues like creative control and representation. Many artists and musicians face significant challenges when it comes to protecting their rights, and may be forced to make difficult choices between their artistic vision and financial stability.

Ensuring fair compensation and the protection of rights for artists and musicians requires action from across the industry. This can include initiatives such as fair trade agreements, transparent and equitable contracts, and increased support for independent artists and musicians. It also requires a shift in cultural attitudes, specifically a greater recognition of the value and importance of artistic and musical work.

CONCLUSION

As we come to the end of this book, I hope you've gained a deep appreciation for the art and science of music production. We've explored a wide range of topics, from the technical aspects of digital audio workstations to the creative process of composing and arranging music. We've also discussed the business side of music production, including marketing strategies, financial management principles, and ethical considerations.

Throughout the book, our message has been clear: music production is a complex and rewarding field that requires both technical skill and artistic vision. Whether you're a seasoned professional or a newcomer to the industry, there's always more to learn and discover.

As we recap some of the key takeaways from the book, remember that every aspect of music production is interconnected. From the initial idea to the final mix, every decision you make has an impact on the final product. By paying close attention to the details and approaching each project with creativity and dedication, you can create music that resonates with listeners and stands the test of time.

Some of the most important topics we've covered include the role of technology in music production, the importance of fair compensation and rights for artists and musicians, and the need for diversity and inclusivity within the industry.

So, what is the one thing I want you to take away from this book? Simply put, it's that music production is an endlessly fascinating and rewarding field that offers countless opportunities for creative expression and personal growth. By applying the principles and techniques we've discussed, you can create music that not only sounds great, but also has the power to inspire and connect with others.

In closing, I want to thank you for taking the time to read this book. I hope that it has provided you with valuable insights and practical tips that you can apply in your own music production endeavors. Remember that there's always more to learn and discover, so keep exploring and creating, and never stop making music.

REFERENCES

MUSIC PRODUCTION FOR BEGINNERS | 2024+ EDITION

Adobe. (2023). Best audio format file types | Adobe. Www.adobe.com. https://www.adobe.com/creativecloud/video/discover/best-audio-format.html

Audiosorcerer. (2022, December 12). What Is Audio Clipping And Is It Always A Bad Thing? Audio Sorcerer. https://www.audiosorcerer.com/post/what-is-audio-clipping

AWAL. (2019, April 30). Decoded: The History of Record Deals. AWAL. https://www.awal.com/blog/history-of-record-deals/

Butler, S. (2022, June 23). 6 Best Apps to Auto-Tune Your Voice. Online Tech Tips. https://www.online-tech-tips.com/software-reviews/6-best-apps-to-auto-tune-your-voice/

Buzzsprout. (2022, March 6). How to Use the Compressor in Audacity. Buzz Sprout. https://www.buzzsprout.com/blog/how-to-use-compressor in-audacity

Christian, R. (2022, September 7). CPU vs. RAM: Understanding the Differences. Computer History. https://history-computer.com/cpu-vs ram/

Clark, B. (2019, October 29). The Loudness War Explained. Musician Wave. https://www.musicianwave.com/the-loudness-war/

Csutoras, B. (2021, July 23). 25 Essential Social Media Marketing Apps for Your Smartphone. Search Engine Journal. https://www.searchenginejournal.com/social-media-marketing-smartphone-apps/257547/

Deviant Noise. (2023, January). Distrokid Review. Deviant Noise. https://deviantnoise.com/music-business/distrokid-review/

Dixon, D. (2019, January 15). What Is the Difference Between Mixing and Mastering? IZotope. https://www.izotope.com/en/learn/what-is-the-difference-between-mixing-and-mastering.html

Fox, Arthur. (2023, March 19). Why Mixing Engineers Use Multiple Pairs Of Studio Monitors. My New Microphone. https://mynewmicrophone.com/why-mixing-engineers-use-multiple-pairs-of-studio-monitors/

Glover, J. (2019, May 28). How to Build an Online Store 2019 | 9 Easy Steps to Start Selling Online. Best Website Builder Reviews for 2019. https://www.websitebuilderexpert.com/building-online-stores/

Grushecky, J. (2022, October 7). Why You Should Record Drums First: The Foundation Of Your Track–grushecky.com. Www.grushecky.com. https://www.grushecky.com/why-you-should-record-drums-first-the-foundation-of-your-track/

Huff, S. (2021, May 7). How To Choose A DAW That Works For You (4 Critical Tips). Producer Hive. https://producerhive.com/buyer-guides/daw/how-to-choose-a-daw/

Lendino, J. (2022, April 6). Audacity Review. PCMAG. https://www.pcmag.com/reviews/audacity

Madden, E. (2019, February 27). From Cher to Bon Iver, via T-Pain, Britney Spears and Kanye West, this is the history of Auto-Tune in seven songs. Red Bull. https://www.redbull.com/us-en/history-of-auto-tune-in-seven-songs

MasterClass. (2022, September 3). Music 101: What Is a Metronome in Music? Learn How to Use a Metronome in 4 Steps. Master Class. https://www.masterclass.com/articles/music-101-what-is-a-metronome-in-music-learn-how-to-use-a-metronome-in-4-steps

McAllister, M. (2021, August 29). The Best Cheap DIY Vocal Booth Options. Produce like a Pro. https://producelikeapro.com/blog/best-inexpensive-diy-vocal-booth/

National Park Service. (2018, July 3). Understanding Sound - Natural Sounds (U.S. National Park Service). Www.nps.gov. https://www.nps.gov/subjects/sound/understandingsound.htm

Paquette, R. (2020, October 23). How much should I spend on Facebook ads? The Revealbot Blog. https://revealbot.com/blog/how-much-should-i-spend-on-facebook-ads/

Pastukhov, D. (2019, January 7). Soundcharts | Market Intelligence for the Music Industry. Soundcharts.com. https://soundcharts.com/blog/mechanics-of-the-music-industry

Pendlebury, T. (2022, December 6). Spotify Review: Still the Best Music Streaming Service. CNET; CNET. https://www.cnet.com/tech/services-and-software/spotify-review-still-the-best-music-streaming-service/

Polner, M. (2022, June 9). How To Start A Podcast And Make Money In 2022. Forbes Advisor. https://www.forbes.com/advisor/business/how-to-start-a-podcast/

Raieli, S. (2023, February 1). Google's MusicLM: from text description to music. Medium. https://towardsdatascience.com/googles-musiclm-from-text-description-to-music-23794ab6955c

Rogerson, B. (2023, February 3). Best DAWs 2023: the best digital audio workstations for PC and Mac. Music Radar. https://www.musicradar.com/news/the-best-daws-the-best-music-production-software-for-pc-and-mac

Science Learn Hub. (2019, September 12). Sound–Visualising Sound Waves. Science Learning Hub. https://www.sciencelearn.org.nz/resources/2814-

sound-visualising-sound-waves

Sgalbazzini, M. (2021, February 1). Why Do You Love "Boring, Repetitive" Electronic Music? 6AM. https://www.6amgroup.com/why-do-you-love-boring-repetitive-electronic-music/

Skaf, E. (2014, December 17). 10 Tips to Avoid Facebook Jail or Being Blocked by Facebook. Postcron - Social Media Marketing Blog and Digital Marketing Blog. https://postcron.com/en/blog/how-to-avoid-being-blocked-by-facebook-jail/

Stewart, D. (2021). Technical GRAMMY Award: Ikutaro Kakehashi And Dave Smith. Grammy.com. https://www.grammy.com/news/technical-grammy-award-ikutaro-kakehashi-and-dave-smith

Sweetwater. (1997, September 10). Sibilance. InSync. https://www.sweetwater.com/insync/sibilance/

Truss, S., & Corfield, C. (2021, February 4). The 9 best budget audio interfaces 2022; start recording today for less than $120/£110. MusicRadar. https://www.musicradar.com/news/best-budget-audio-interfaces

Ward, M. K., Goodman, J. K., & Irwin, J. R. (2013). The same old song: The power of familiarity in music choice. Marketing Letters, 25(1), 1–11. https://doi.org/10.1007/s11002-013-9238-1

MUSIC PRODUCTION | 2024+ EDITION

Allen, J. (2023, March 2). Music production online courses: How to record and mix music. Udemy. https://www.udemy.com/courses/music/production/

Bleu, N. (2023, January 17). 17 best marketing strategies for musicians in 2023. Tone Island. https://toneisland.com/marketing-strategies-for-musicians/

Cortes, Z. (2022, September 27). How to master a song. iZotope. https://www.izotope.com/en/learn/how-to-master-a-song-from-start-to-finish.html

Douglas, P. (2022, June 8). How to start learning a DAW: The best way to learn quickly. Home Music Creator. https://homemusiccreator.com/how-to-start-learning-daw/

Expert Panel. (2020, April 22). 15 financial planning tips for beginners. Forbes. https://www.forbes.com/sites/forbesfinancecouncil/2020/04/22/15-financial-planning-tips-for-beginners/?sh=433569b51bde

Feldman, Z., Ross-Spang, M. & Shoemaker, T. (2022, April 28). How to become a music producer | Job description & salary. Careers in Music | Music Schools & Colleges. https://www.careersinmusic.com/music-producer/

Golden, A. (2001, May). Ethics of the music business and its impact on popular music, society and culture. Victoria University Research Repository. https://vuir.vu.edu.au/188/1/wp5_2001_golden.pdf

Kealey, M. (2021, November 2). 7 top marketing strategies for musicians. Bandzoogle. https://bandzoogle.com/blog/7-top-marketing-strategies-for-musicians

Knight, B. (2022, October 6). What is a DAW: 15 things you can do with it (+ samples). Piano Dreamers. https://www.pianodreamers.com/what-is-daw/

Lake, R. (2022, July 7). A guide to planning your finances. The Balance. https://www.thebalancemoney.com/financial-planning-basics-personal-finance-101-1289798

Landr Blog. (2022, October 13). Music production tips: 15 ideas to help you finish your track. https://blog.landr.com/music-production-tips/

Laukkonen, J. (2021, June 9). What are VST plugins and what do they do? Lifewire. https://www.lifewire.com/what-are-vst-plugins-4177517

Mantione, P. (2020, December 10). 5 strategies for creative discovery in music production. Pro Audio Files. https://theproaudiofiles.com/5-strategies-for-creative-discovery-in-music-production/

Mastering the Mix. (2021, June 29). How to use reverb. https://www.masteringthemix.com/blogs/learn/how-to-use-reverb

Matla, S. (2023, March 9). 38 essential tips for new music producers. EDMProd. https://www.edmprod.com/38-essential-tips/Messitte, N. (2022, May 12). What is the difference between mixing and mastering? iZotope. https://www.izotope.com/en/learn/what-is-the-difference-between-mixing-and-mastering.html

Music-production-guide.com. (2019). The music production process. https://www.music-production-guide.com/music-production-process.html

Nostairway.com. (2021, April 27). Music production and how has it evolved over the years. https://www.nostairway.com/music-production/

The O2. (2016). 8 technological advances that changed the music industry forever | The O2. https://www.theo2.co.uk/news/detail/blog_8_technological_advances_that_changed_the_music_industry_forever

Reinholdt, E. (2017, September 7). How to design the perfect home music studio. Electronic House. https://www.electronichouse.com/home-audio/how-to-design-the-perfect-home-music-studio/

Rory PQ. (2020, May 27). Being an independent artist vs. signing to a record label. Icon Collective. https://iconcollective.edu/independent-artist-vs-signed-artist/

Rouse, M. (Ed.). (2015, March 6). Virtual studio technology. Techopedia. https://www.techopedia.com/definition/266/virtual-studio-technology-vstSerenade Team. (2022, May 2). Discover how new tech is changing the music industry in 2022. Serenade Magazine.

https://serenademagazine.com/discover-how-new-tech-is-changing-the-music-industry-in-2022/

DISCOVER "HOW TO FIND YOUR SOUND"

https://www.subscribepage.com/tsmusic

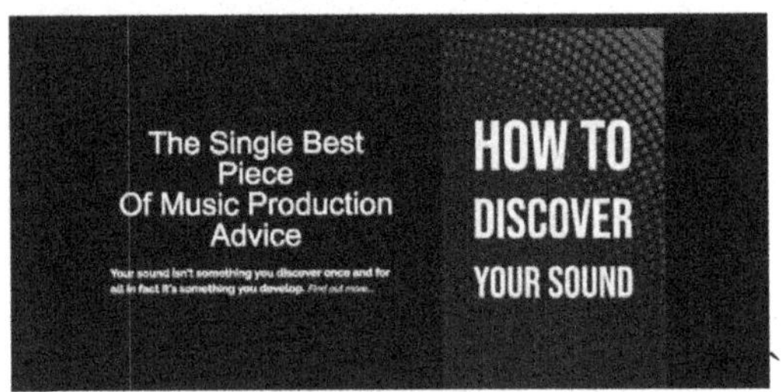

Scan the QR code for more.

OTHER BOOKS BY TOMMY SWINDALI

Scan the QR code with your smartphone to be taken to a truly amazing collection of books by Tommy Swindali!

CONNECT WITH ME HERE

www.tommyswindali.com

www.swindali.com

Made in the USA
Monee, IL
03 January 2024